LOTUS LEAVES

# THE DOCTRINE OF THE HEART

## EXTRACTS FROM HINDU LETTERS

WITH A FOREWORD BY

## ANNIE BESANT

**London:**
**The Theosophical Publishing Society,**
**3, Langham Place, W.**

NEW YORK AGENCY, 67, FIFTH AVENUE.
BENARES: THE THEOSOPHICAL PUBLISHING SOCIETY.
MADRAS: THE "THEOSOPHIST" OFFICE, ADYAR.

1899.

# FOREWORD

---

LEARN to discern the real from the false, the
ever-fleeting from the ever-lasting.  Learn, above
all, to separate Head-learning from Soul-wisdom,
the " Eye " from the " Heart " doctrine.—*Voice of
the Silence*.

UNDER the title of THE DOCTRINE OF
THE HEART are here printed a series of
papers, consisting chiefly of extracts of
letters received from Indian friends.  They
are not given as being of any " authority,"
but merely as containing thoughts that
some of us have found helpful, and that
we wish to share with others.  They are
intended only for those who are resolutely
seeking to live the Higher Life, and are
addressed to those especially who know
that this life leads to a definite entering
on the Path of Discipleship under the

Great Ones who trod it in the past, and who remain on earth to help others to tread it in their turn. The thoughts in these letters are thoughts that belong to all religions, but the phrases and the sentiment are Indian. The devotion is of that noble and intense kind known in the East as Bhakti—the devotion that surrenders itself wholly and unreservedly to God and to the Divine Man through whom God is manifest in the flesh to the devotee. This Bhakti has nowhere found more perfect expression than in Hinduism, and the writers of these letters are Hindus, accustomed to the luxuriant richness of the Sanskrit, and tuning the harsher English into some faint harmony with the poetical sweetness of their mother-tongue. The chill and reserved dignity of the Anglo-Saxon and his emotional reticence are wholly alien from the out-flowing of religious feeling that wells up from the Eastern heart as naturally as song from the lark.  Here and there in the West we find a true Bhakta [devotee], such as S. Thomas à Kempis, S. Theresa, S. John of the Cross, S. Francis of Assisi, S. Elisabeth of Hungary.  But for the most part, religious feeling in the West, however deep and true, tends to silence and seeks to hide itself.  To those who shrink from the expression of religious feeling these letters will not be helpful, and for them they are not intended.

Let us now turn to the consideration of one of the marked contrasts of the Higher Life.  We have all of us recognised the fact that Occultism makes on us demands of a character which necessitates a certain isolation and a rigid self-discipline.  Both from our much-loved and revered Teacher, H. P. B., and from the traditions of the Occult Life, we have learned that renunciation and stern self-control are required from him who would pass through the gateway of the Temple. *The Bhagavad*

*Gîtâ* constantly reiterates the teaching of indifference to pain and pleasure, of the perfect balance under all circumstances, without which no true Yoga is possible. This side of the Occult Life is recognised in theory by all, and some are obediently striving to mould themselves into its likeness. The other side of the Occult Life is dwelt upon in *The Voice of the Silence*, and consists of that sympathy with all that feels, that swift response to every human need, the perfect expression of which in Those we serve has given Them as title "The Masters of Compassion." It is this, in its practical, every-day aspect, to which these letters direct our thoughts, and it is this which we overlook most in our lives, however much the beauty of it, in its perfection, may touch our hearts. The true Occultist, while he is to himself the sternest of judges, the most rigid of taskmasters, is to all around him the most sympathising of friends, the gentlest of helpers. To reach this gentleness and power of sympathy should, then, be the aim of each of us, and it can only be gained by unremitting practice of such gentleness and sympathy towards all, without exception, who surround us: Every would-be Occultist should be the one person, in his own home and circle, to whom everyone most readily turns in sorrow, in anxiety, in sin—sure of sympathy, sure of help. The most unattractive, the most dull, the most stupid, the most repellent, should feel that in him, at least, they have a friend. Every yearning towards a better life, every budding desire towards unselfish service, every half-formed wish to live more nobly, should find in him one ready to encourage and strengthen, so that every germ of good may begin to grow under the warming and stimulating presence of his loving nature.

To reach this power of service is a

matter of self-training in daily life.   First
we need to recognise that the SELF in all
is one ; so that in each person with whom
we come in contact, we shall ignore all
that is unlovely in the outer casing, and
recognise the SELF seated in the heart.
The next thing is to realise—in *feeling*,
not only in theory—that the SELF is en-
deavouring to express itself through the
casings that obstruct it, and that the inner
nature is altogether lovely, and is distorted
to us by the envelopes that surround it.
Then we should identify ourselves with
that SELF, which is indeed ourself in its
essence, and co-operate with it in its warfare against the lower elements that stifle
its expression.   And since we have to
work through our own lower nature on
the lower nature of our brother, the only
way to effectually help is to see things *as
that brother sees them*, with his limitations,
his prejudices, his distorted vision ; and
thus seeing them, and being affected by

them in our lower nature, help him in his
way and not in ours, for thus only can
real help be given. Here comes in the
Occult training. We learn to withdraw
ourselves from our lower nature, to study
it, to feel its feelings without being thereby affected, and so while emotionally we
experience, intellectually we judge.

We must utilise this method for our
brother's help, and while we feel as he
feels, as the synchronised string gives out
the note of its fellow, we must use our
disengaged " I " to judge, to advise, to
raise, but always so using it that our
brother shall be conscious that it is *his*
better nature that is uttering itself by our
lips.

We must desire to share our best ; not
to keep, but to give, is the life of the
Spirit. Often our " best " would be unattractive to the one we are trying to help,
as noble poetry to a little child ; then we
must give the best he can assimilate,

withholding the other, not because we grudge it, but because he does not yet want it. Thus do the Masters of Compassion help us who are as children to Them, and in like fashion must we seek to help those who are younger than we are in the life of the Spirit.

Nor let us forget that the person who happens to be with us at any moment is the person given to us by the Master to serve at that moment. If by carelessness, by impatience, by indifference, we fail to help him, we have failed in our Master's work. We often miss this immediate duty by absorption in other work, failing to understand that the helping of the human soul sent to us *is* our work of the moment; and we need to remind ourselves of this danger, the subtler because duty is used to mask duty, and failure of insight is failure in accomplishment. We must not be attached even to work of any particular description; always at work indeed, but with the soul free and " at attention," ready to catch the slightest whisper from Him, who may need from us service of some helpless one whom, through us, He wills to help.

The sternness to the lower self, spoken of above, is a condition of this helpful service; for only the one who has no cares of his own, who is for himself indifferent to pleasure and pain, is sufficiently free to give perfect sympathy to others. Needing nothing he can give everything. With no love for himself, he becomes love incarnate to others.

In Occultism the book of life is the one to which we turn our chief attention. We study other books merely in order that we may live. For study even of Occult works is only a means to spirituality if we are striving to live the Occult Life; it is the life and not the knowledge, the purified heart, not the well-filled head, that leads us to our Master's Feet.

The word " devotion " is the key to all true progress in the spiritual life. If in working we seek the growth of the spiritual movement and not gratifying success, the service of the Masters and not our own self-gratulation, we cannot be discouraged by temporary failures, nor by the clouds and deadness that we may experience in our own inner life.

To serve for the sake of service, and not for the pleasure we take in serving, is to make a distinct step forward, for we then begin to gain that balance, that equilibrium, which enables us to serve as contentedly in failure as in success, in inner darkness as in inner light. When we have succeeded in dominating the personality so far as to feel real *pleasure* in doing work for the Master which is painful to the lower nature, the next step is to do it as heartily and fully when this pleasure disappears and all the joy and light are clouded over. Otherwise in serving the Holy Ones we may be serving self—serving for what we get from Them, instead of for pure love's sake.

So long as this subtle form of self-seeking prevails, we are in danger of falling away from service if darkness remain long around us, and if we feel dead inside and hopeless. It is in this night of the spirit that the noblest service is rendered, and the last snares of the lower self are broken through.

We lay this stress on devotion, because everywhere we find that aspirants are endangered, and the progress of the Master's work is hindered, by the predominance of the personal self. Here is our enemy, here our battle-ground. Once seeing this, the aspirant should welcome everything in his daily life that chips a bit off the personality, and should be grateful to all the " unpleasant persons " who tread on his toes and jar his sensibilities and ruffle his self-love. They are his best friends, his most useful helpers, and should never be regarded with anything but gratitude for the services they render in bruising our most dangerous enemy. Looking thus on daily life, it becomes a school of Occultism, and we begin to learn that perfect balance which is required in the higher walks of discipleship, ere deeper knowledge, and therefore power, can be placed in our hands. Where there is not calm self-mastery, indifference to personal matters, serene devotion to work for others, there is no true Occultism, no really spiritual life. The lower psychism demands none of these qualities, and is, therefore, eagerly grasped at by pseudo-Occultists; but the White Lodge demands these of its postulants, and makes their acquirement the condition of entrance into the Neophytes' Court. Let the aim of every aspirant be, therefore, to train himself that he may serve, to practise stern self-discipline that "when the

Master looks into the heart He may see no stain therein." Then will He take him by the hand and lead him onward.

ANNIE BESANT.

# THE DOCTRINE OF THE HEART

---

DISASTER hangs over the head of the man who pins his faith on external paraphernalia rather than on the peace of the inner life, which depends not on the mode of the outer life. In fact, the more untoward the circumstances, and the greater the sacrifice involved by living among them, the nearer does one come to the final goal from the very nature of the trials one has to overcome. It is unwise, therefore, to be attracted too much by any outward manifestation of religious life, for anything that is on the plane of matter is ephemeral and illusive, and must lead to disappointment. Anyone who is drawn powerfully to any external modes of living has to learn sooner or later the comparative insignificance of all outer things. And the sooner one passes through experiences necessitated by past Karma the better it is for the individual. It is unwelcome indeed to be suddenly thrown off one's ground, but the cup which cures folly is ever bitter, and must be tasted if the disease is to be eradicated. When the gentle breeze coming from Their Lotus Feet blows over the soul, then you know that the worst external surroundings are not powerful enough to mar the music that charms within.

Just as a European who is drawn to Occultism feels nearer to the Great Ones when he lands in India, so does an Indian feel when he ascends the heights of his snowy Himavat. And yet it is quite an illusion, for one approaches not the Lords of Purity by physical locomotion, but by making oneself purer and stronger through constant suffering for the welfare of the world. As for the ignorance of the poor deluded world regarding our revered Lords, I am reminded of the words: "The hissing of the serpent does more harm to the sublime Himavat, than the slander and abuse of the world to any of us."

* * *

IF it be once admitted, as it must be by all who have any knowledge of Occultism, that there are hosts of invisible agencies constantly taking part in human affairs, Elementals and Elementaries of all grades breeding all sorts of illusion and masquerading in all garbs, as well as members of the Black Lodge who delight in gulling and deluding the votaries of true wisdom—one must also recognise that Nature, in her great mercy and absolute justice, must have endowed man with some faculty to discriminate between the voices of these aërial denizens and that of the Masters. And I fancy that it will be agreed on all hands that reason, intuition

and conscience are our highest faculties,
the only means by which we can know the
true from the false, good from evil, right
from wrong. That being so, it follows
that nothing which fails to illuminate the
reason and satisfy the most scrupulous
claims of the moral nature should ever be
regarded as a communication from the
Masters.

It must also be remembered that the
Masters are the Masters of Wisdom and
Compassion, that Their words illumine
and expand, never confound and harass
the mind; they soothe, not disturb; they
elevate, not degrade. Never do They use
methods which wither and paralyse reason and intuition alike. What would be
the inevitable result if these Lords of Love
and Light were to force on Their disciples
communications revolting equally to the
reason and the ethical sense? Blind credulity would take the place of intelligent
faith, moral palsy instead of spiritual

growth would ensue, and the Neophytes would be left quite helpless, with nothing to guide them, constantly at the mercy of every frolicsome nymph, and worse still, of every vicious Dugpa.

Is this the fate of discipleship? can such be the way of Love and Wisdom? I do not think that any reasonable man can believe it for any length of time, although for a moment a glamour may be thrown upon him and he may be made to swallow the veriest absurdities.

AMONG the many doubts thrown into the mind of the disciple to cause him distress, is the doubt whether physical weakness may be a bar to spiritual progress. The process of assimilation of spiritual nourishment involves no drain upon physical energies, and spiritual progress can go on while the body suffers. It is an entire fallacy, due to lack of knowledge and of balance, to suppose that the torture and starvation of the body make it responsive to *spiritual* experiences. It is by doing that which best serves the purpose of the Holy Ones that steady and real progress is made. When the right time comes for spiritual experiences to be impressed on the brain-consciousness, the body cannot stand in the way. The little difficulty that can be raised by the body can be swept away in a second. It is a delusion that any physical effort can advance spiritual progress by a single step. The way to approach Them is to do that which best furthers Their wish, and this done, nothing else needs to be done.

*\* \* \**

IT seems to me that there is a peculiar sweetness in being resignedly patient, in gladly sacrificing one's own will to the will of Those who know better and always guide aright. There is no such thing as personal wish in the life of the Spirit. So the disciple may gladly sacrifice his own

personal bliss, while They find occasion to
work through him for others.   He may
sometimes feel as though forsaken when
he is alone, but he will always find Them
at his side when work has to be done.
Periods of night must alternate with those
of day, and it is surely well that darkness
should come at a time when it affects
ourselves alone, even though our personal
pain should be thereby intensified.    To
feel Their presence and influence is indeed
the divinest gift imaginable, but even that
we should be willing to sacrifice, if by re-
nouncing what we deem the highest and
best, the final good of the world be made
easier of attainment.

\*   \*
\*

TRY and realise the beauty of suffering,
when suffering only makes one better
fitted for work.   Surely we can never
crave for peace if in strife the world must
be helped.   Try and feel that though darkness seems to be all round you, yet it is

*not* real. If They sometimes veil Themselves in an outer Mâyâ of indifference, it is but to shed Their blessings with greater luxuriance when the season is ripe. Words avail not much when the darkness is overshadowing, yet the disciple should try to keep unshaken his faith in the nearness of the Great Ones, and to feel that though the light is temporarily withdrawn from the mind-consciousness, yet, under Their wise and merciful dispensation, it is growing daily within. When the mind again becomes sensitive, it recognises with surprise and joy how the spiritual work has gone on without its having had any consciousness of the details. We know the Law. In the spiritual world nights of greater or less horror invariably follow the day, and the wise one, recognising the darkness to be the outcome of a natural law, ceases to fret. We can rest assured that the darkness, in its turn, will lift. Remember always that behind the thickest

smoke is ever the light from the Lotus
Feet of the Great Lords of the earth.
Stand firm and never lose faith in Them,
and there is then nothing to fear. Trials
you may, and indeed must, have, but you
will be sure to withstand them. When
the darkness that hangs like a pall over
the Soul lifts, then we are able to see how
really shadowy and illusive it was. Yet
this darkness, as long as it lasts, is real
enough to bring ruin to many a noble soul
that has not yet acquired strength enough
to endure.

\* \* \*

SPIRITUAL life and love are not ex-
hausted by being spent. Expenditure
only adds to the store and makes it richer
and intenser. Try and be as happy and
contented as you can, because in joy is
the real spiritual life, and sorrow is but
the result of our ignorance and absence
of clear vision. So you should resist, as
much as you can, the feeling of sadness;

it clouds the spiritual atmosphere.  And
though you cannot entirely stop its coming, yet you should not altogether yield
to it.  For remember that at the very
heart of the universe is Beatitude.

DESPAIR should find no room in the
heart of the devoted disciple, for it
weakens faith and devotion, and thus
furnishes an arena for the Dark Powers to
wrestle in.  The feeling is a glamour cast
by them to torture the disciple, and if
possible to reap some advantage for themselves out of the illusion.  I have learned
from the bitterest experience that self-
reliance is quite unavailing and even deceptive under trials of this nature, and the
only way to escape unscathed from these
illusions is to devote oneself completely
to Them.  The reason of this, too, is
plain enough.  The force, in order to be
effective in its opposition, must be on the

same plane as that on which the power to be counteracted plays. Now as these troubles and illusions come not from the self, the self is powerless against them. Proceeding as they do from the Dark Ones, they can only be neutralised by the White Brothers. Therefore it is necessary for safety to surrender ourselves—our separated selves—and to be freed from all Ahamkâra.

\*  
\*   \*

KNOWING as we do that our Society[1]—or, for the matter of that, every movement of any consequence—is under the watch and ward of vastly wiser and higher Powers than our little selves, we need not concern ourselves much about the ultimate destiny of the Society, but rest content with doing our duty by it conscientiously and diligently, playing the part assigned to us according to our best light

[1] The Theosophical Society

and abilities.   Care and solicitude have,
no doubt, their own functions in the economy of Nature.   In ordinary men they
set the brains to work, and even the
muscles to motion, and were it not for
these the world would not make half the
progress it has done on the physical and
intellectual planes.   But at a certain stage
of human evolution these are replaced by
a sense of duty and a love of Truth, and
the clearness of vision and impetus to
work thus attained can never be furnished
by any amount of molecular energy and
nervous vigour.   Therefore shake off all
despondency, and with your Soul turned
towards the Fountain of Light work on to
that great end for which you are here,
your heart embracing all mankind, but
perfectly resigned as to the result of your
labours.   Thus have our Sages taught,
thus did SHRĪ KRISHNA exhort Arjuna on
the battle-field, and thus shall we direct
our energies.

MY own feelings with regard to the suffering of the world are precisely the same as yours. There is nothing which pains me more than the blind and frantic manner in which a vast majority of our fellow-beings pursue the pleasures of the senses, and the utterly blank and erroneous view they take of life. The sight of this ignorance and madness touches my heart much more tenderly than the physical hardships that people undergo. And although Rantideva's noble prayer moved me deeply years ago, with the glimpse that I have since been allowed into the inner nature of things, I regard the BUDDHA's sentiments as wiser and more transcendental. And though I would gladly suffer agony to relieve a disciple of the torture to which he is subjected, yet having regard to the causes as well as the intimate consequences of a disciple's sufferings, my grief for them is not half so intense as it is for the misery of those ignorant wretches who *unintelligently* pay the mere penalty of their past misdeeds.

\* \* \*

THE functions of intellect are merely comparison and ratiocination; spiritual knowledge is far beyond its scope. You are probably quite surfeited with intellectual subtleties in your present surroundings; but the world is, after all, only a school, a training academy, and no experience, however painful or ridiculous, is without its uses and value to the thoughtful man. The evils that we come across only make us wiser, and the very blunders we make serve us in good stead for the future. So we need not grumble at any lot, however outwardly unenviable.

\* \* \*

KARMA, as taught in the *Gîtâ* and the *Yoga Vâsishṭha*, means acts and volitions proceeding from Vâsanâ, or desire. It is distinctly laid down in those ethical codes that nothing done from a pure sense of

duty, nothing prompted by a feeling of
" oughtness," so to say, can taint the
*moral nature* of the doer, even if he be mistaken in his conception of duty and pro-
priety.   The mistake, of course, has to be
expiated by suffering, which must be pro-
portionate to the consequences of the error;
but certainly it cannot degrade the character or tarnish the Jivâtmâ.[1]

*  *  *

IT is well to use all the events of life
as lessons to be turned to advantage, and
the pain caused by separation from friends
we love may thus be used.   What are
space and time on the plane of the Spirit?
Illusions of the brain, nonentities merely,
acquiring a semblance of reality from the
impotency of the mind, the involucra
which imprison the Jivâtmâ.   The suffering merely gives a fresh and more potent
impulse to live altogether in the Spirit.

---

[1] The individualised Self.

Good will come in the end to every one of us out of the pain, and so we must not murmur. Nay, knowing that to disciples nothing of any consequence can happen which is not the will of their Lords, we must look upon every painful incident as a step towards spiritual progress, as a means to that inner development which will enable us to serve Them, and hence Humanity, better.

\* \* \*

IF we can but serve Them, if through all storms and conflagrations our Souls turn to Their Lotus Feet, what matter the pain and the sufferings that these inflict on our transitory wrappings? Let us understand a little of the inner meanings of these sufferings, these vicissitudes of outer circumstances—how so much pain endured means so much bad Karma worked out, so much power of service gained, such a good lesson learned—are not these thoughts sufficient to support us through any amount of these illusory miseries? How sweet it is to suffer when one knows and has faith; how different from the wretchedness of the ignorant, and the sceptic, and the unbeliever. One could almost wish that all the suffering and misery of the world were ours, in order that the rest of our kind might be liberated and be happy. The crucifixion of Jesus Christ symbolises this phase of the disciple's mind. Do you not think so? Only be always firm in faith and devotion, and swerve not from the sacred path of Love and Truth. This is your part—the rest shall be done for you by the Merciful Lords you serve. You know all this, and if I speak of it, it is only to strengthen you in your knowledge; for we often forget some of our best lessons, and in times of trouble the duty of a friend is more to remind you of your own sayings than to inculcate new truths. Thus it is that Draupadî often consoled her sage husband Yudhisṭhira when dire misfortune would for a moment overthrow his usual serenity, and thus Vasishṭha himself had to be soothed and comforted when torn with the pangs of his children's death. Truly unspeakable is the Mâyâ side of this world! how beautiful and romantic on the one hand, and yet how horrible and wretched on the other. Yes, Mâyâ is the mystery of all mysteries, and one who has understood Mâyâ has found his own unity with BRAHMAN—the Supreme Bliss and the Supreme Light.

\* \* \*

THE startling picture of Kâlî standing on the prostrate SHIVA is an illustration of the utility—the higher use—of Anger and Hatred. The black complexion represents Anger; with the sword it also means physical prowess; and the whole figure means that so long as a man has anger and hatred and physical strength he should use them for the suppression of the other passions, the massacre of the desires of the flesh. It also represents what really happens when first the mind turns towards the higher life. As yet we are wanting in wisdom and in mental equilibrium, and so we crush our desires with our passions ; our anger we direct against our own vices, and thus suppress them ; our pride also we employ against the unworthy tendencies of the body and mind alike, and thus gain the first rung of the ladder. The prostrate SHIVA shows that when one is engaged in a warfare like this, he pays no heed to his highest principle, the Âtmâ—nay, he actually tramples upon it, and not until he has slain the last enemy of his Self does he come to recognise his actual position during the fight with regard to the Âtmâ. Thus, Kâlî finds SHIVA at her feet only when she has killed the last Daitya, the personification of Ahamkâra, and then she blushes at her insane fury. So long as the passions have not all been subdued, we must use them for their own suppression, neutralising the force of one with that of another, and thus alone can we at first succeed in killing out selfishness, and in catching the first glimpse of our true Âtmâ—the SHIVA within us—which we ignore while desires rage in the heart.

*  *  *

WELL may we always lay aside our own short-sighted personal wish in order to serve Them faithfully; it is my experience that in thus following Their guidance alone one always avoids some dangerous precipice against which one was unconsciously running. For the moment it seems hard to break away from one's likings, but in the end nothing but joy results from such sacrifice. There is no training better than the few brief years of one's life when one is driven by sheer disappointment to seek shelter under the blessed Feet of the Lords, for nowhere else is there room for rest. And then there grows in the disciple a habit of thinking always that his only refuge is in Them, and whenever he thinks not of Them he feels miserable and forlorn. Thus from the very darkness of despair burns out for him a light that never afterwards grows dim. Those whose eyes penetrate the stretches of the far-off future, which are veiled from our mortal eyes, have done and will do what is best for the world. Immediate results and temporary satisfactions must be sacrificed, if the end is to be secured without a chance of failure. The stronger we desire to make the chances of ultimate success, the less should we crave for the reapings of the day. Only by pain can we attain to perfection and purity; only by pain can we make ourselves fit servants of the Orphan that cries incessantly for food spiritual. Life is only worth having as it is sacrificed at Their Feet.

LET us rejoice that we have opportunities of serving the great Cause by personal sacrifices, for such suffering can be used by Them to draw the poor erring Humanity a little step higher. Any pain that a disciple may suffer is an earnest for a corresponding gain that comes to the world. He should, therefore, suffer ungrudgingly and gladly, since he sees a little more clearly than the blind mortality for which he suffers. In the whole course of evolution there is one law that is only too painfully evident, even to the eyes of the merest tyro, that nothing that is really worth having can be obtained without a corresponding sacrifice.

\* \* \*

HE who resigneth all sense of self, and maketh himself an instrument for the Divine Hands to work with, need have no fear about the trials and difficulties of the hard world. " As Thou directest, so I work." This is the easiest way of passing outside the sphere of individual Karma, for one who layeth down all his capacities at the Feet of the Lords creates no Karma for himself; and then, as SHRÎ KRISHNA promises: "I take upon Myself his balance of accounts." The disciple need take no thought for the fruits of his actions. So taught the great Christian Master: "Take no thought for the morrow."

\* \* \*

Do not allow impulses to guide conduct. Enthusiasm belongs to feeling, not to conduct. Enthusiasm in conduct has no place in real Occultism, for the Occultist must be always self-contained. One of the most difficult things in the life of the Occultist is to hold the balance evenly, and this power comes from real spiritual insight. The Occultist has to live more an inner than an outer life. He feels, realises, knows, more and more, but shows less and less. Even the sacrifices he has to make belong more to the inner world than to the outer. In ordinary religious devotion all the sacrifice and strength one's nature is capable of are used in adhering to externals, and in overcoming ridicule and temptations on the physical plane. But these have to be used for grander objects in the life of the Occultist. Proportion must be considered, and the external subordinated. In a word, never be peculiar. As the Hamsa takes the milk alone and leaves the water behind from a mixture of both, so doth the Occultist extract and retain the life and quintessence of all the various qualities, while rejecting the husks in which these were concealed.

\* \* \*

How can people suppose that the Masters ought to interfere with the life and actions of people, and argue for Their non-existence, or for Their moral indifference, because They do not interfere? Folk might with equal reason question the existence of any moral Law in this Universe, and argue that the existence of iniquities and infamous practices among mankind is against the supposition of such a Law. Why do they forget that the Masters are Jîvanmuktas and work with the Law, identify themselves with the Law, are in fact the very spirit of the Law? But there is no need to be distressed over this, for the tribunal to which we submit in matters of conscience is not public opinion but our own Higher Self. It is battle such as this that purifies the heart and elevates the soul, and not the furious fight to which our passions, or even "just indignation," **and** what is termed "righteous resentment," impel us.

*  *  *

WHAT are troubles and difficulties to us? Are they not as welcome as pleasures and facilities? For are they not

our best trainers and educators, and re-
plete with salutary lessons? Does it not
then behove us to move more evenly
through all changes of life and vicissitudes of fortune? And would it not be
much to our discredit if we failed in pre-
serving the tranquillity of mind and
equilibrium of temper which ought always to mark the disposition of the disciple? Surely he should remain serene
amid all external storms and tempests.
It is a mad world this, altogether, if one
looks at the mere outside of it, and yet
how deceptive in its madness! It is the
true insanity of lunacy where the subject
of the disease is ignorant of his condition
—nay, believes himself perfectly sound.
Oh! if the harmony and the music which
reign within the Soul of things were not
perceptible to us, whose eyes have been
opened to this utter madness that per-
vades the outer shell, how intolerable life
would be to us.

Do you not think that it is not quite grateful to be cheerless, when we are obeying the wishes of our Lords and are out on our duty? You should not only have peace and contentment but also joy and liveliness, while you are serving Those whose service is our highest privilege and the memory of whom is our truest delight.

\* \* \*

THAT They will never desert us is as certain as Death. But it is for us to cling to Them with real and deep devotion. If our devotion be real and deep there is not the remotest chance of our falling away from Their holy Feet. But you know what real and deep devotion means. You know just as well as I do that nothing short of complete renunciation of the personal will, the absolute annihilation of the personal element in man, can constitute Bhakti proper and genuine. It is only when the *whole* human nature is in perfect harmony with the Divine Law, when there is not one discordant note in any part of the system, when all one's thoughts, ideas, fancies, desires, emotions voluntary or involuntary, vibrate in response to and in complete concord with the " Great Breath," that the true ideal of devotion is attained, and not till then. We only rise beyond the chance of failure when this stage of Bhakti is reached, which alone ensures perpetual progress and undoubted success. The disciple does not fail through lack of care and love on the part of the Great Masters, but in spite of these, and through his own perverseness and inborn weakness. And we cannot say that perverseness is impossible in one who has yet lingering in him the idea of separateness—ingrained through æons of illusive thought and corruption, and not yet completely rooted out.

\*  \*  \*

WE must not delude ourselves in any way. Some truths are indeed bitter, but

the wisest course is to know them and
face them. To dwell in a fancied para-
dise is only to shut off the real Elysium.
It is true that if we sit down deliberately
to find out whether or not we have still
any trace of separateness or personality
left in us, any wish to counteract the
natural course of events, we may fail to
find any motive, any reason, for such self-
assertion or wish. Knowing and believ-
ing as we do that the idea of isolation is a
mere product of Mâyâ, that ignorance and
all personal desires flow only from this
feeling of isolation and are the root of
all our misery, we cannot but scout these
false and illusory notions when reasoning
upon or about them. But if we analyse
the actual facts, and watch ourselves all
the day, and observe the various modes of
our being, varying with the different circumstances, a very different conclusion
will press itself upon us, and we shall find
that the actual realisation in our own life

of our knowledge and belief is yet a far-
off incident and comes only for a brief
moment now and again, when we are entirely forgetful of the body or any other
material environment, and are completely
wrapped in the contemplation of the
Divine—nay, are merged in the Deity
Himself.

\* \*
\*

To us, through the supreme mercy of
our Lords, things on earth are a little
plainer and more intelligible than to the
man of the world, and that is why we are
so eager to devote all our life's energy to
Their service. All activity—charity, bene-
volence, patriotism, etc.—a cynic will say
with jubilant sneer, is mere barter, is a
pure question of give and take. But the
nobler aspect which even this jeered-at,
mercantile honesty—strictly construed
and applied to higher walks of life—pre-
sents to the higher eye, is beyond the ken
of the supercilious mocker; and so he

laughs at and scouts honesty, calling it
mercantile, and the foolish and light-
hearted world, thirsting for a little mirth,
laughs with him and calls him a shrewd
and witty fellow.   If we look at the surface of this wonderful sphere of ours, nothing but sadness and gloom will over-
spread our souls, and despair will paralyse
all efforts at bettering its condition.   But,
looking beneath, how all inconsistencies
melt away, and everything appears beautiful and harmonious, and the heart blooms
and is gladdened, and liberally opens its
treasures to the surrounding universe.  So
we need not feel disheartened at any
frightful sight we see, nor mourn over the
madness and the blindness of the men
amidst whom we are born.

* * *

THERE are fixed moral laws, just as
there are uniform physical laws.  These
moral laws may be violated by man, endowed as he is with individuality and the

freedom which that involves.   Each such
violation becomes a moral force in the
direction opposite to that towards which
evolution is drifting, and inheres in the
moral plane.   And by the law of reaction
each has a tendency to evoke the operation of the right law.   Now, when these
opposing forces accumulate and acquire a
gigantic form, the reactionary force necessarily becomes violent and results in
moral and spiritual revolutions, pious
wars, religious crusades, and the like.
Expand this theory and you understand
the necessity for the appearance of Ava-
târas on earth.   How easy things become
when one's eyes are opened ; but how in-
comprehensible they look when the spiritual vision is blind, or even dim and dull.
Nature in her infinite bounty has provided
man on the outer planes with exact fac-
similes of her inner workings, and verily
those who have eyes to see may see, and
those who have ears to hear may hear.

How intense is the longing to carry aid
to the suffering Soul, in its hours of dire
trial and of dreary darkness.    But experience shows those who have passed through
similar ordeals, that it is well that they did
not at such times perceive the aid that yet
is always given, and that they were weighed
down with a sad sense of loneliness and of
being totally forlorn.    Were it otherwise,
half the effect of the trial were lost, and
the strength and knowledge which follow
every such ordeal would have to be acquired by years of groping and tottering.
The law of Action and Reaction is everywhere operative.  .  .  .    One whose
devotion is complete, *i.e.*, one who in deed
as well as in thought consecrates all his
energies and all his possessions to the
Supreme Deity, and realises his own
nothingness as well as the falsity of the
idea of separateness—such a one alone is
not allowed to be approached by the
powers of darkness, and is protected from

every danger to his Soul.   The passage in
the *Gîtâ* you are thinking of must be in-
terpreted to mean that no one who has
the feeling of devotion once awakened in
him can fall away *for ever*.   But there is
no guarantee for him against temporary
aberrations.   Why, in one sense, every
living being from the highest Angel to the
meanest protozoon is under the protec-
tion of the LOGOS of his or its system, and
is carried through various stages and
modes of existence back to His bosom,
there to enjoy the blessedness of Moksha
for an eternity.

* * *

THE *without* always reveals the *within*
to the seeing eye, and places and people
are therefore always interesting.   Again,
the *without* is not such a despicable thing
as one may fancy in the first intensity and
acuteness of his Vairâgya, or disgust with
shows.   For if it were so, all creation
would be a folly and a purposeless expen-

diture of energy.   But you know that it is
not so in fact; that on the other hand
there is a deep and sound philosophy even
in these illusory manifestations and outward vestures, and that Carlyle in his
*Sartor Resartus* has shadowed forth a portion of this philosophy.   Why then turn
with sickness and horror from even the
outermost garbage?   Are not even the
robes in which the Supreme Deity mas-
querades holy to us and full of wise
lessons?   You say rightly that all things,
fair and foul, have their suitable places in
Nature, and constitute by their very
difference and variety the perfection of
the Supreme Logos.

*   *   *

WHY should communication with the
inside world be cut off, causing sadness
and heaviness of heart?   Because the
outside has still some lessons to teach,
and one of these lessons is that it also is
divine in its essence, divine in its sub-

stance, and divine in its methods, and
that therefore you should take more kindly
to it. On the other hand, sadness and
melancholy have their use and philosophy.
They are as much needed for the evolution and budding out of the human Soul
as joy and liveliness. They are, however,
needed only at the earlier stages of our
growth, and are dispensed with when the
Self has blossomed out and has opened
its heart to the Divine Sun.

\* \* \*

You know how evolution works. We
begin with no sensation at all. Gradually
we develope it, and at one point of our
pilgrimage we have it in the intensest degree. Then comes a period in which
sensation is looked upon as Mâyâ, and
thus it begins to diminish and knowledge
predominates, until in the end all sensation is burned up by knowledge, and we
have absolute peace. But not peace in
nescience, as at the commencement of our

life in the mineral kingdom, but peace in
omniscience—peace, not in complete
apathy and as it were death, such as we
see in stones, but in absolute life and absolute love.   This finds rest, because it
enlivens all that is, and pours its blessings
upon the whole Universe.   But extremes
meet, and so in one of the aspects the beginning and the end coincide.

*  *  *

Two points I want to make clear : (1)
That untrained psychics always run the
risk of putting forward things really said
by the enemy as injunctions from the
Master ; and (2) That the Master says
nothing that the intellect of His audience
cannot grasp, and against which their
moral sense revolts.   Master's words, however much they may be opposed to one's
previous thoughts, never fail to bring the
most absolute conviction, alike to the intellect and to the moral sense of the person addressed.   They come like a revela-

tion, rectifying an error which becomes at once apparent; they stream down like a column of light dispelling the gloom; they make no claim on credulity or blind faith.

*  *  *

You know how the enemy has been working against us, and if we fail in our devotion to Masters, or in the discharge of the duties with which They have been pleased to entrust us, he will give us no end of trouble. But these troubles we do not much mind; we can endure them quite patiently and without a ruffle. What does torture us and disturb the peace of our mind, is the tearing away from our Lords with which we are now and again threatened. Nothing else can torment us—no personal pain, no physical loss, however great their amount. For we know beyond all doubt that all that is personal is transitory and fleeting, and all that is physical is illusory and false, and that nothing but folly and ignorance mourn over things belonging to the world of shadows.

\* \* \*

For the disciple little is gained from teaching on the intellectual plane. The knowledge that infiltrates from the Soul down into the intellect is the only knowledge worth having, and surely as the days roll by the disciple's store of such knowledge increases. And with the increase of such knowledge comes about the elimination of all that hinders him on the Path.

\* \* \*

The feeling of pain is one to which any person who leads the life of the Spirit becomes accustomed. We know that pain cannot last for ever, and even if it did it would not matter very much. We cannot hope to be of any service to Them or to Humanity without taking our full measure of suffering from the enemies. But the ire of these Monarchs of Darkness is

sometimes terrible to face, and they perfectly startle one by the Mâyâ they sometimes create. But a pure heart has nothing to fear and is sure to triumph.
The disciple must not distress himself
over the temporary pain and illusion they
try to create. Sometimes they may seem
to work a regular havoc inside, and then
he has to sit upon the ruins of himself,
quietly waiting for the time when the
âsuric Mâyâ shall pass away. Always he
should allow the wave of doubt and unrest
to sweep over him, holding firmly to the
anchor he has found. The enemy can do
him no real or substantial harm, so long
as he remains devoted to Them with all
his Soul and with all his might. "He
who clingeth to Me easily crosseth the
ocean of death and of the world, by My
help."

\* \*
\*

NOTHING can happen to the disciple but
that which is best for him. Once a person

deliberately puts himself into the Hands
of the gracious Masters, They see that
everything happens at the proper time—
the time at which the greatest advantage
is reaped, alike for the disciple and for the
world.   He should therefore take all that
comes in his way with a contented and
cheerful spirit, and " take no thought for
the morrow." . . . The storm-tossed
bark on a raging sea is more peaceful than
the life of the pilgrim to the shrine of
Spirit.   A peaceful life would mean stag-
nation and death in the case of one who
has not acquired the right to peace by
completely destroying the enemy—personality.

\* \*
\*

You should not fall into fallacies that
are committed by the ignorant.   All real
Love is an attribute of the Spirit, and
Prânâ and Bhakti are the two aspects of
the Divine Prakriti (Nature) which go to
make worth living the life of an aspirant

after the waters of immortality. In the stormy darkness of the disciple's life the sole light comes from Love, for Love and Ânanda (Bliss) are in the highest sense identical, and the purer and the more spiritual the Love the more does it partake of the nature of Ânanda, and the less is it mixed with incongruous elements. Only the Masters' holy love is so majestically serene as to have nothing in it that does not partake of the Divine.

DISCRETION and economy are quite as necessary in Occultism as anywhere else. In fact, in the life of the Occultist all the faculties of the human mind that are regarded as virtues in the ordinary sense are put to the greatest use and exercise, and are necessary adjuncts to the real life which alone makes a disciple. The world cannot be helped so easily as many imagine, even if there were more agents available for the work. Knowledge on the part of the disciple is not the only thing needed. Look out and ponder, ere deciding that the knowledge and devotion of the few can push on the hands of the clock. Not a single attempt can be made without provoking fierce hostility from the other side, and is the world prepared to survive the reaction? You will understand how wise are our Lords in not going further than They do, if you only learn from all you have seen.

* * *

WHAT would life be worth if we did not suffer—suffer to render the world groaning under our eyes a little purer, suffer to win a little more of the waters of life that will quench the thirst of some parched lips? In fact, but for the suffering that is the fate of the disciple who walks with bleeding feet on the Path, he might stray away and lose sight of the goal on which his gaze must ever be fixed. The Mâyâ of the phenomenal world is so confusing, so bewitching, that it seems to me that the elimination of the pain must inevitably be followed by oblivion of the realities of existence, and with the disappearance of the shadow of spiritual life its light would vanish too. So long as man has not been transformed into God, it is vain to expect to be in uninterrupted enjoyment of spiritual bliss, and in periods of its absence suffering alone keeps the feet of the disciple steady, and saves him from the death which would surely overtake him in the forgetfulness of the verities of the spiritual world.

* * *

THE disciple should not be disturbed nor surprised when the spiritual forces turned against him by the other side find their playground on a plane higher than that of the physical intellect. It is true that the dying embers in some unseen and unnoticed cranny of his own nature may be fanned thereby into flame; but the flame is one that forms the signal of the final destruction of some weakness that must be burned away. So long as the taint of personality has not been clean washed out, vice in its manifold forms may find shelter in some neglected chamber of the heart, though it may not find expression in mental life. And the only way to render the sanctuary of the heart immaculate is to let the search-light pierce into dark crannies, and calmly witness the work of their destruction. The disciple must never let this purificatory process fill him with dismay, whatever monstrosities he may be called upon to witness. He must hold fast to the Feet of Him who dwells in the glorious burning-ground of all that is material ; then he has nothing to fear or to be anxious about. He has faith in Those who protect and help, and may well leave the workings on the spiritual plane to be watched and directed by Them. When the dark cycle is over, he will again recognise how the gold shines when the dross has been burned away.

\* \* \*

IN this mundane sphere of ours, as on all planes of existence, night alternates with day—there is shadow beneath the lamp itself. And yet how strange that men of culture and erudition should fancy that with the advancement of Science, of gross materialistic Science, all misery, individual, racial, and national, will cease for ever and ever; diseases, droughts, plagues, wars, inundations, nay, cataclysms themselves will all be things of the remote past !

\* \* \*

THE interest that we have in all the affairs of this elusive sphere belongs only to the emotions and the intellect, and cannot touch the Soul. So long as we identify ourselves with the body and the mind, the vicissitudes which overcome the Theosophical Society, the dangers which threaten its life or solidarity, must have a depressing, nay, sometimes almost a frenzied, influence upon our spirits. But as soon as we come to live in the Spirit, to *realise* the illusory nature of all external existence, the changeful character of every human organisation, and the immutability of the Life within, we must, whether the brain-consciousness reflect the knowledge or not, feel an inward calm, an unconcernedness, as it were, with this world of shadows, and remain unaffected by the revolutions and eruptions of the world. Once the Higher Ego is reached, the knowledge that the Laws and Powers which govern the universe are infinitely wise becomes instinctive, and peace in the midst of outward throes is inevitable.

* * *

ROUGHLY and broadly speaking, on the plane we live upon there are three standpoints of looking at human misery in general. We may regard it, for instance :

(1) As a test of character; (2) as a retributive agency; and (3) as a means of education in the largest signification of that word. From all these points of view, I fancy the " deadness " (experienced by all aspirants at times) stands to acute pain in very much the same relation as solitary confinement to imprisonment with hard labour. The illustration is, no doubt, a very crude one, but it seems to me very suggestive, and I have invariably found analogy to be of great help in the comprehension of abstract and subtle propositions ; hence this plan of explaining things. Again, all the forces here are working towards the evolution of perfected humanity, and it is only by the harmonious development of all our higher faculties and nobler virtues that we can attain perfection. And this harmonious development is possible only by the proper exercise of those faculties and virtues, while this exercise in its turn requires

*particular conditions* for each distinct attribute. *Positive* intense suffering does
not either test or repay or bring into play
the same capacities and merits of mankind
as a dull, dreary void within. Patience,
passive endurance, faith, devotion, are far
better developed under a mental gloom
than during an active, hard struggle. The
law of action and reaction holds good on
the moral plane, and the virtues evoked
by this mental " numbness " are those
best fitted to combat and overcome it ; and
these are certainly not the same with which
you confront actual pain, however ex-
cruciating. One word more on this point,
and I shall pass on. This state of mind
indicates that the pilgrim is on the border-
land between the known and the unknown,
with a distinct tendency towards the
latter. It marks a definite degree of spiritual growth, and points to that stage where
the Soul in its onward march has,vaguely,
yet unmistakably, realised the illusive

E

character of the material world, is dissatisfied and disgusted with the gross things it sees, and knows and hankers after things more real, knowledge more substantial.

The above explanation, though very succinct and desultory, will, I hope, satisfy you as to the utility of vairâgya—of the feeling of the absence of all life and reality in both yourself and the world around you—in the economy of Nature, and show how it serves as a touchstone for firmness of mind and singleness of heart, how as a punitive measure it antidotes intellectual egoism—the philosophical blunder of identifying the Self with the personality—the folly of seeking to nourish the Soul with gross material food; and how, moreover, it developes, or rather tends to develope, true faith and devotion, and awakens the higher Reason and the Love of the Divine.

\* \* \*

FROM the highest to the lowest, life is

an alternation between rest and motion, between light and darkness, between pleasure and pain. So never allow your heart to sink into despair or to be carried away by any adverse current of thought. You have proved to yourself intellectually, and are now actually experiencing, the shadowy, unreal character of things perceptible by the organs of sense or even by the mind, and the ephemeral nature of all physical and emotional enjoyments. Hold fast, therefore, to the path which will bring you to a view of the real life, however rugged the regions through which it leads, however destitute of joy the deserts across which it now and then winds. Above all, have faith in the Merciful Ones, our Wise Masters, and devote yourself heart and soul to Their service, and all will come out well.

\* \* \*

ALL that is needed for the weeding out of any vice is :

(1) An accurate knowledge of the vice itself;

(2) A recognition—a keen feeling, that it is a *vice*, that it is foolish to entertain it, and that it is worthless; and, lastly,

(3) The will to " kill it out."

This *will* will penetrate into the subconscious sphere where the vice dwells, and slowly but surely erase it.

*  *  *

REAL tranquillity of mind is never the product of indifference and nonchalance, but can only proceed from an insight into higher and deeper wisdom.

*  *  *

A DISCIPLE, however humble, of Their High Lodge, has to live in the Eternal, and his life must be a life of Universal Love, or else he must abandon his higher aspirations. The active service which every disciple has to do to the world is different for different classes of students, and is determined by the peculiar nature, disposition, and capacity of the individual. You of course know that, so long as perfection is not achieved, variety has to be maintained even in the mode of service a chelâ must render.

*  *  *

IT is simply impossible to over-estimate the efficacy of Truth in all its phases and bearings in helping the onward evolution of the human Soul. We must love Truth, seek Truth, and live Truth ; and thus alone can the Divine Light, which is Truth Sublime, be seen by the student of Occultism. Where there is the slightest leaning towards falsehood in any shape there is shadow and ignorance, and their child, pain. And this leaning towards falsehood belongs to the lower personality without doubt. It is here that our interests clash, it is here that the struggle for existence is in full sway, and it is therefore here that cowardice and dishonesty and fraud find any scope.

THE "signs and symptoms" of the operation of this lower self can never remain concealed from one who sincerely loves Truth and seeks Truth and has devotion to the Great Ones at the foundation of his conduct. Unless the heart be perverse, doubts as to the righteousness of any particular act will never fail to find articulation, and then the true disciple will ask himself: "Will my Master be pleased if I do such and such a thing?" or, "Was it at His bidding that I moved in this way?" And the true answer will soon come up, and then he will learn to mend his ways and harmonise his wishes with the Divine Will and thereafter attain to wisdom and peace.

\* \* \*

THEOSOPHY is not a thing which can be thrust and hammered *nolens volens* into anybody's head or heart. It must be assimilated with ease in the natural course of evolution, and inhaled like the air around us.   Otherwise it will cause indigestion, to use a vulgar expression.

*  *  *

BEGINNING to feel the growth of one's Soul, one realises the calm that no outward events seem to touch.   This, again, is the best proof of spiritual development, and one who feels this, however slightly and vaguely, need not care for any Occult phenomena.   From the very beginning of my novitiate I have been taught to rely more upon the calm within than upon any phenomena on the physical, astral, or spiritual planes.   And, given favourable conditions and strength in oneself, the less one sees of phenomena, the easier it is to make real and substantial spiritual progress.   So my humble advice to you is to devote your attention ever to growing calm within, and not to wish to know in detail the process by which the growth is effected.   If you are patient, pure and devoted, you will know all in time, but remember always that perfect and resigned contentment is the soul of spiritual life.

\* \* \*

SPIRITUAL progress is not always the same as goodness and self-sacrifice, although these must in due season bring about the former.

\* \* \*

IT is true that there is in the desire to win the affection of people around one, a tinge of personality which, if eliminated, would make one an angel ; but one has to remember that for a long, long time to come our actions will continue to be tinged slightly with a feeling of " self." It must be our constant endeavour to kill this feeling as far as possible, but so long as " self " must show itself in some way, it is much better that it should exist as an inappreciable factor in conduct which is gentle, affectionate and conducive to general welfare, than that the heart should be hardened, the general character rendered angular, the "self" manifesting itself in far less attractive and lovely colours. By this I do not for a moment suggest that efforts should not be made in washing out this faint stain, but what I mean to convey is that the soft and lovely drapery in which the mind clothes itself should not be cast into the fire, simply because it is not one of immaculate whiteness. We have to bear in mind that all our actions are more or less the result of two factors, a desire for self-gratification, and a wish to benefit the world—and our constant effort should be to attenuate as far as is possible the former element, since it may not, till the germ of personality ceases to exist, be completely eliminated. That germ can be killed by processes which the disciple learns as he progresses, by devotion and good actions.

\* \*<br>\*

THE Masters are always near those of Their servants who by complete self-

abnegation have devoted themselves body,
mind, and soul to Their service. And
even a kind word to these does not go
unrequited. In times of severe trial
They, in accordance with a beneficent
law, let the disciple fight his or her own
battle without help from Them; but anyone who encourages Their servant to stand
firm has his reward without a doubt.

\* \* \*

KEEPING serene and passionless, there
is no doubt that, as the days pass by, one
is coming more and more within that influence which is the essence of life, and
some day the disciple will be surprised to
find he has grown wonderfully without
knowing and perceiving the process of
growth. For truly the Soul, in its true
blooming, " grows like the flower, unconsciously," but gaining in sweetness
and beauty by imbibing the sunshine of
Spirit.

A COMBATIVE loyalty to any person or cause is hardly commendable in a disciple, and is certainly no indication of spiritual progress.

* * *

THE first step, in almost every case, has the effect of disturbing a nest of hornets. All the odd items of your evil Karma crowd around you thick and fast, and would make one with less steady feet feel giddy and shaky. But one, whose whole object is to lay down, if it need be, his life for the sake of others, without caring for self, has nothing to fear. The very jolting in the ups and downs of this vortex of miseries and trials gives one strength and confidence. and forces the growth of the Soul.

* * *

REMEMBER that the suffering a disciple has to undergo is an integral portion of his training, and flows out of his desire to crush the personality in him. And, at the end, he will find the flower of his Soul blooming the more charmingly for the storm it has braved, and the love and mercy of the Master more than compensating for all he has suffered and sacrificed. It is only a trial for the moment, because at the end he will find he has sacrificed nothing and gained all.

\*\*\*

Love on the highest plane reposes on the serene heights of joy alone, and nothing can cast a shadow on its snowy eminence.

\*\*\*

Pity and compassion are the proper feelings to cherish in respect to all erring humanity, and we must not give place to any other emotion, such as resentment, annoyance, or vexation. These latter may not only injure ourselves, but also those against whom we may chance to entertain them, but whom we would fain see bettered and freed from all blunders. As

we grow spiritually, our thoughts grow
incredibly stronger in dynamic power,
and none but those who have actual experience know how even a passing thought
of an Initiate finds objective form.

*  *  *

IT is wonderful how the Powers of the
Dark seem to sweep away, as it were, in
one gust all one's richest spiritual treasures,
garnered with such pain and care after
years of incessant study and experience.
It is wonderful, because after all it is an
illusion, and you find it to be one so soon
as the peace is restored and light dawns
upon you again.   You see that you have
lost nothing—that all your treasures are
there, and the storm and the loss are all
a chimera.

*  *  *

HOWEVER heart-rending the outlook
may at any time be, however gloomy and
dreary the state of things, we must not for
one single moment give room to despair ;

for despair weakens the mind and thus renders us less capable of serving our Masters.

\* \* \*

KNOW for certain that the Lords of Compassion are always watching their true devotees, and never allow honest hearts and earnest seekers for light to remain under an illusion for any length of time; the Wise Lords bring out of even their temporary recessions lessons which serve them in good stead through the rest of their lives.

\* \* \*

IT is simply our ignorance and blindness that give the appearance of strangeness and unintelligibleness to our work. If we come to view things in their true light and in their full and deeper significations, all will appear perfectly just and fair, and the most perfect expression of the highest reason.

THAT there is in the order of manifested existence not a whit more pain and misery than is absolutely necessary for the ends of the highest evolution, follows directly from the law of Justice and Compassion —the law of Karma and the moral government of the Universe. That each act of self-sacrifice on the part of evolving human monads strengthens the hands of the Masters and brings reinforcement, as it were, to the Powers of Goodness will also be made plain ere we are things of the past—at least to a great many of the present race.

*
* *

IT would not avail us much if we knew accurately in detail all that was going to happen to us. For we are not concerned with results, and all we should care about is our own duty ; so long as the path is clear to us it is of little consequence what comes of the steps we take on this outer plane. It is the inner life that is the real life; and if our faith in the guidance of our Lords be firm, we ought to have no doubt that whatever the appearances in this illusory sphere may be, all shall go well within, and the world shall go forward on its line of evolution. There is comfort enough in this idea, there is blessedness enough in this thought, and this alone should suffice to nerve us to our present duties and stimulate us to further activity and harder work.

\* \* \*

THERE is a great difference between one who knows the spiritual life to be a reality and the man who only babbles about it but perceives it not, who clutches at and grasps for it, but inhales not its fragrant breath nor feels its exquisite touch.

\* \* \*

THERE is far more wisdom in Those who are watching over us than we have any conception of, and if only we can firmly pin our faith on this we shall not fall into any blunders, and shall be sure to avoid much unnecessary and worse than useless worry. For not a few of our mistakes might be traced to excess of anxiety and fear, to overstrung nerves, and even to too much zeal.

*  *  *

You will now see that whole-hearted devotion is a potent factor in promoting the growth of the Soul, although it be not seen and realised for the moment ; and you will not blame me for having told you to leave aside all thought about phenomena and spiritual knowledge, psychic power and abnormal experiences. For in the serene sunlight of peace every flower of the Soul smiles and grows rich in its peculiar radiant dye. And then some day the disciple looks with amazement at the beauty and delicious fragrance of every flower, rejoices, and in the rejoicing knows that the beauty and radiance emanate from the Lord he has served. The pro-

D

cess of growth is not the hackneyed detestable article known to dabblers in pseudo-Occultism. It is a thing mysterious; so sweet, so subtle that none may speak of it, but may only *know* by service.

* * *

You have tasted some drops of the ambrosial waters of Peace, and in the tasting have found strength. Know now and for ever that in the calm of the Soul lies real knowledge, and from the divine tranquillity of the heart comes power. Experience of celestial peace and joy is therefore the only true spiritual life, and growth in peace alone means growth of the Soul. The witnessing of abnormal phenomena by the physical senses can but arouse curiosity and not promote growth. Devotion and peace form the atmosphere in which the Soul doth live, and the more you have of those the more life your Soul will possess. Rely always therefore on the experiences of your Higher Self as a

test of your own progress, as also of the
reality of the spiritual world, and do not
attach any importance to physical phenomena which never do, never can, form the
source of strength and comfort.

*\* \* \**

THE humble and devoted servants of the
Masters really form a chain by which each
link is held to the Compassionate Ones.
The tightness of the hold of one link to
the one next in advance to it, therefore
implies the strength of the chain which
ever draws us up to Them. Hence one
should never fall into the popular fallacy
of regarding the love which partakes so
largely of the divine as a weakness. Even
ordinary love, if it be real, deep and self-
less, is the highest and purest manifestation of the Higher Self, and if entertained
in one's bosom with constancy and desire
of self-sacrifice, ultimately brings one to a
clearer realisation of the spiritual world
than does any other human act or

emotion. What then of a love which has for its basis a common aspiration to reach the Throne of God, a joint prayer to suffer for the ignorant and erring humanity, and a mutual pledge to sacrifice one's own happiness and comfort for the better rendering of service to Those who are ever building a bulwark with Their blessings between the terrible forces of evil and the defenceless orphan—Humanity. . . . But the ideas of the world are all distorted by the selfishness and baseness of human nature. If in love there be weakness, I do not know where lies strength. *Real* strength does not consist in strife and opposition, but lies all-potent in love and inner peace. So the man who cares to live and grow must ever love, and suffer for love.

*  *  *

WHEN has the world, blind in its ignorance and self-conceit, done full justice to its real saviours and most devoted servants ?    It is enough that one sees, and in that seeing attempts to dispel to what extent may be possible the delusion of the people around one.    The wish that everyone should have the eyes to see and to recognise the Power that works for his regeneration must remain unfulfilled, till the present darkness that hangs like a pall obscuring the spiritual vision has been lifted completely.

PEACE TO ALL BEINGS.

Women's Printing Society, Ltd., 66, Whitcomb St., W.C.

# The Path of Discipleship

FOUR LECTURES DELIVERED AT THE TWENTIETH
ANNIVERSARY OF THE THEOSOPHICAL SOCIETY,
AT ADYAR, MADRAS, DECEMBER 27, 28, 29
AND 30, 1895

BY
ANNIE BESANT

*EIGHTH REPRINT*

Theosophical Publishing House
KROTONA
HOLLYWOOD, LOS ANGELES, CAL.
*Reprinted 1918*

# CONTENTS

# THE PATH OF DISCIPLESHIP

## FIRST STEPS

### KARMA-YOGA. PURIFICATION

BROTHERS:—When first I spoke in this Hall two years ago, I led your attention to the building of the Kosmos as a whole, to the steps through which that evolution took place, the methods, as it were, of the vast succession of phenomena. Last year I dealt with the evolution of the Self, the Self in man rather than the Self in the Kosmos, and tried to show you how from sheath after sheath the Self gained experience and obtained sovereignty over its lower vehicles—still with the man as with the universe, still with the individual as with the Kosmos, seeking ever reunion with the Self, seeking ever That whence it had come. But sometimes men have said to me when discussing these lofty topics: "What bearing have these on the life of men in the world, surrounded as we are with the necessities of life, surrounded as we are with the activities of the phenomenal world, continually drawn away from the thought of the one Self, continually forced by our Karma to take part in these multifarious activities? What bearing then has the

higher teaching on the lives of men, and how may
men in the world rise upward until the higher
life becomes possible also for them?''  It is that
question that I am going to try to answer this
year.  I am going to try to show you how a man in
the world, surrounded with family obligations,
with social duties, with all the many activities of
worldly life, may yet prepare himself for union
and take the first steps on the path that leads him
to the One.  I am going to try to trace for you the
steps of that path, so that beginning in the life that
any man may be leading, starting from the standpoint where most of you may be standing at the
moment, you may recognize a goal to be reached,
you may recognize a path to be trodden—the path
which begins here in the life of the family, of the
community, of the state, but which ends in that
which is beyond all thinking and lands the traveller
ultimately in the home which is his for evermore.
Such is the object then of these four lectures, such
the steps along which I trust you will accompany
me; and in order that we may understand our subject let us glance for a moment at the course of
evolution, at its meaning, at its object, so that from
what must be but a bird's-eye view of the whole,
we may be able, appreciating the whole, to understand the congruity of the steps which one by one
we are to take.  We realize that the One has become the many.  Glancing backward into the primal
darkness that shrouded all, we can hear out of that

darkness but a whisper—a whisper: "I will multiply." That multiplication is the building of the universe, and of the individuals who live within it. In that will to multiply of the "One which is without a second," we see the source of manifestation, we recognize the primal germ, as it were, of the Kosmos. And as we realize that beginning of the universe and as we see the complexity, the multiplicity, that result from the primal simplicity, from the primal unity, we realize also that in each of these phenomenal manifestations there must be imperfection, and that the very limitation which makes a phenomenon possible is also the inevitable mark that it is less than the One, and therefore by itself imperfect. So we understand why there should be variety, why there should be this vast multiplicity of separate and living things. And we begin to understand that the perfection of the manifested universe must needs lie in this very variety; that if there be more than the One then there must be well-nigh infinite multiplicity, in order that the One, which is as a mighty sun sending forth beams of light in all directions, may send beams everywhere, and in the totality of the beams will be the perfection of the lighting of the world. The more numerous, the more wonderful, the more various the objects, the more nearly, though still imperfectly, will the universe image forth That whence it comes.

The first effort in the evolving life must be to

make many, to make separated existences—apparently separate—so that looked .at from without there shall seem many, although looked at in their essence we see that the Self of all is One. Realizing that, we understand that in the process of multiple individualization, the one as individual comes into manifestation as a faint and limited reflection of the Self. And we begin to understand also what is to be the outcome of this universe, why it is that these many individuals should be evolved, why it is that this separateness should be a necessary part in the evolution of the whole. For we begin to see that the result of the universe is to be the evolution of the LOGOS of another universe, of the mighty Devas who are to be the guides of all the kosmic forces of that universe in the future, and of the divine Teachers whose duty it will be to train the infant humanity of another Kosmos. What is going on today in all these worlds of individual existences is a steady process of evolution, by which one universe gives to a future universe its LOGOS, its Devas, the earliest of its Manus, and all those great Ones that will be necessary for the building, for the training, for the governing, for the teaching of the universe which is yet unborn. Thus are the universes linked together, thus does Manvantara succeed Manvantara, thus are the fruits of one universe the seeds of the universe that succeeds it. In the midst of all this multiplicity there is being evolved a yet vaster unity which shall be the framework of the unborn Kosmos, which shall be the Power which in the future Kosmos shall guide and rule.

And then the question arises—as I know it arises in many minds, for it has been put to me both in the East and in the West over and over again—why so much difficulty in the evolution, why so much apparent failure in the working, why should men go wrong so much before they go right, why should they run after the evil that degrades them instead of following the good that would ennoble them? Was it not possible for the LOGOS of our universe, for the Devas who are His Agents, for the great Manus who came to guide our infant humanity—was it not possible for Them to plan so that there might be no such apparent failure in the working out? Was it not possible for Them to guide so that the road might have been a straight and direct one instead of so devious, so circuitous?

Here comes the point that makes the evolution of humanity so difficult, having in view the object which is to be gained. Easy in truth would it have been to have made a humanity that might have been perfect, easy to have so guided its dawning powers that those powers might have travelled towards what we call the good continually, and never have turned aside towards what we call evil. But what would have been the condition of such an easy accomplishment? It must have been that man would have been an automaton, moved by a com-

pelling force without him which imperiously laid
upon him a law which he was compelled to fulfil,
from which he could not escape. The mineral world
is under such a law; the affinities that bind atom
to atom obey such an imperious compulsion. But
as we rise higher we find greater and greater freedom gradually making its appearance, until in
man we see a spontaneous energy, a freedom of
choice, which is really the dawning manifestation
of the God, of the Self, which is beginning to show
Itself through man. And the object, the goal which
was to be attained, was not to make automata who
should blindly follow a path sketched out for their
treading, but to make a reflection of the Logos
Himself, to make a mighty assemblage of wise and
perfected men who should choose the best because
they know and understand it, who should reject
the worst because by experience they have learnt
its inadequacy and the sorrow to which it leads. So
that in the universe of the future, as amongst all
the great Ones who are guiding the universe of to-
day, there should be unity gained by consensus of
wills, which have become one again by knowledge
and by choice, which move with a single purpose
because they know the whole, which are identical
with the Law because they have learned that the
Law is good, which choose to be one with the Law
not by an outside compulsion, but by an inner ac-
quiescence. Thus in that universe of the future
there will be one Law, as there is in the present,

carried out by means of Those who are the Law by
the unity of Their purpose, the unity of Their
knowledge, the unity of Their power—not a blind
and unconscious Law, but an assemblage of living
beings who are the Law, having become divine.
There is no other road by which such goal might
be reached, by which the free-will of the many
should reunite into the one great Nature and the
one great Law, save a process in which experience
should be garnered, in which evil should be known
as well as good, failure as well as triumph. Thus
men become Gods, and because of the experience
that lies behind them, they will, they think, they
feel, the same.

Now in working towards this goal the divine
Teachers and Guides of our humanity planned
many civilizations, all moulded towards the end
that was in view. I have no time to go back to the
great civilization of the Fourth Race that preceded
the birth of the mighty Âryan people. I may only
say in passing that there was a great civilization
which was tried, which for a time under its divine
Rulers succeeded; then the divine Rulers withdrew their immediate guiding—as a mother withdraws her hand from her babe that is learning to
walk, in order to see if without her supporting
arm it is able to make its own steps, it is able to
use its own limbs, so for the same purpose They
withdrew into the darkness—the divine Guides
and Rulers—to see if the child-humanity making

these early steps would walk or would stumble on its way. And that infant humanity stumbled and fell, and the great civilization—mighty as it was perfect in its social order, glorious in the strength and the wisdom by which it was builded—broke into pieces under the selfishness of man, broke into pieces under the yet unconquered lower instincts of humanity. Another attempt had to be made, and the great Âryan race was founded—again with divine Rulers, again with divine Guides, with a Manu who gave it its law, founded its civilization, sketched out its polity, with the Rishis who gathered around Him, who administered His laws and guided the infant civilization; thus again humanity was given a pattern, again the race was shown a type towards which it should evolve. Then once more the great Teachers drew back for awhile to let humanity again try its own strength, again experiment if it were strong enough to walk alone, self-reliant, guided by the Self from within, instead of by outer manifestations. And again, as we know, the experiment has largely been a failure. Again, as we know, glancing backward, we see this civilization originally divine gradually degenerating under the still unconquered lower nature of man, again going downward for awhile under the still uncurbed passions of humanity. Looking back, as we now do, to the India of the past, we see its perfect polity, its marvelous spirituality, and we trace its degradation millennium after millennium as the guiding hand withdraws out of the visible sight of man, and once more humanity blunders and fails as it tries to walk. We see how in each case there has been the failure of the realization of the divine ideal. We glance over the modern world and we see how the lower nature of man has triumphed over the divine ideal which was set before him at the beginning of the Aryan race. We see how in that day there was the ideal of the Brâhmana, an ideal that might be summed up as that of the soul approaching liberation, which asks no longer for the goods of earth, which asks no longer for the enjoyments of the flesh, which asks no longer for the gifts of wealth, of power, of authority, of earthly pleasure, the type of the Brâhmana being that he was poor, but wise; whereas today we too often find the man who bears the Brâhmana name not poor and wise but wealthy and ignorant. There in that caste you have one of the signs of the degeneration by which the ancient polity fell; and the same with each of the four castes.

Let us now see how it was proposed by the great Teachers that man by experience should learn to choose of his own free will the ideal which was placed before him, and from which he turned aside: how the great Teachers endeavored to build up from the imperfect humanity towards the perfected ideal manifested in the beginning for the guidance of the race, and unrealized in evolution by the weakness and the childishness of men.

In order that, in the course of ages, this might be achieved, what is called Karma-Yoga was taught to the people—Yoga, or union, by action. That is the form of Yoga which is fitted for the men of the world, beset with life's activities; it is by these very activities, by the training afforded by them, that the first steps towards union must be taken. And so you find laid down for the training of men this Karma-Yoga.

Note the juxtaposition of the words "action" and "union." Action so performed that union may result, action so carried out that union may be the outcome. It is a thing to remember that it is our activities that divide us, it is our actions that separate us, it is all this changing and multifarious activity by which we are drawn and kept apart. It seems almost a paradox then to speak of union by action, union by that which was ever a means of division, union by that by which separation was brought about. But the wisdom of the divine Teachers was equal to the task of reconciling, of explaining, the apparent paradox. Let us follow the steps of the explanation and see what it is.

Man runs wild, runs wild in every direction, under the influence of the three energies in nature, the gunas. The dweller in the body finds himself under the domination of these gunas. They are at work, they are active, they make the manifested

universe, and he identifies himself with these activities. He thinks he is acting when these are acting. He thinks he is busy when these are bringing
about results. Living amongst them, blinded by
them, under the illusions which they produce, he
loses entirely all recognition of himself, and is
taken here and there, blown hither and thither,
carried away by the currents, and so the activity
of the gunas is all that the man sees in life; clearly
he is not fit under these conditions for the higher
forms of Yoga. Clearly until these illusions are
at least partially conquered the loftier steps on the
Path will be beyond his treading. He must begin
then by understanding the gunas, by separating
himself from these activities of the phenomenal
universe. And the great scripture of Yoga, as it
may be called, the scripture of this Karma-Yoga, is
that which was re-proclaimed by Shrî Krishna on
the field of Kurukshetra, when he taught this form
of Yoga to Arjuna, to the prince, to the warrior,
the man who was to live in the world, to fight in
the world, to rule the state, and take part in all
external activities; here is the eternal lesson for
men who are living in the world, how gradually
they may rise beyond the gunas and so reach union
with the Supreme.

It will then first be in what we may call the
training and regulation of the activities of the
gunas that this Karma-Yoga will consist. There
are, as you know, three gunas, Sattva, Rajas and

Tamas, the three gunas out of which all around us is builded and combined together in various ways, mingled in various fashions. Here one is acting and the other is working in every direction. They have to be brought into equilibrium; they have to be reduced to subjection. The dweller in the body, the lord of the body, must become sovereign master and distinguish himself from the gunas. That, then, will be the work that has to be done; their functions must be realized, their activities must be controlled and directed. You cannot at once rise above them, you cannot at once cross beyond them —any more than a child can do the work of a full-grown man. Can humanity in its unevolved and in its imperfect state accomplish perfection of Yoga? Nay, it is not even wise that man should try; for if the child be put to the work of the full-grown man, he will not only fail to accomplish it, but he will overstrain his powers in the attempt, and the result will be not only failure in the present, but also failure in the future. For the task too great for his powers will thwart and distort them. They must be trained to strength before they can accomplish, and the child must grow to manhood before manhood's work should be his. Take for a moment the function of Tamas—translated darkness, or sluggishness, or inertia, or negligence, and so on. What function can that play, if it is to be used for human evolution? What use has this particular guna in the growth of the man, in the liberating of the soul? The particular use of that guna, the use to which it will be put in Karma-Yoga, is to act as a force which is to be struggled against and overcome, so that strength may be evolved in the struggle, power of will may be developed by the effort, self-control and self-discipline may be accomplished by the attempt. It may be said to serve in the evolution of man as the club or dumb-bell serves the purpose of the athlete. He could not strengthen his muscles unless there was something against which he exercised them. He could not gain muscular vigor unless there were opposing weights by struggling to lift which the muscles should grow strong. The value is not in the weight itself, but in the use to which it is put, and if a man wants his physical muscles, the muscles of his arms, to grow very strong, the best way to strengthen them is to take a club or dumb-bell and daily exercise the muscles against that opposing force. In this way Tamas, negligence or darkness, plays its part in the evolution of the man; he has to overcome it, he develops his strength in the struggle; the muscles of the soul grow powerful as he overcomes negligence, the sloth, the indifference which is the tâmasic quality in his nature.

So you will find for the overcoming of these the rites and ceremonies of religion are ordained, part of their function being to train man to overcome the sloth and the laziness and the indolence of his lower nature, and by placing before him certain duties to be done at a particular time—whether at that time he is inclined to do them or not, whether at that time he is feeling active or feeling lazy— by imposing on him duties at a particular time he is trained to overcome the sloth and heedlessness and obstinacy of his lower nature and to compel it to walk along the path that the will has determined it should follow.

And so if we take Rajas; you will find the activities of man are guided in Karma-Yoga along certain definite paths which I now propose to follow, so that you may see how this quality of activity, which is so much at work in the modern world, which is manifesting itself in every direction, which leads to hurry, bustle and constant effort to accomplish things in the lower life, material manifestations, material results, material phenomena— how this shall be gradually directed, trained and purified until it no longer has the power to hinder the real manifestation of the Self. The object of Karma-Yoga is to substitute duty for self-gratification; man acts to gratify his lower nature; he acts because he wants to get something; he acts for fruit; he acts for desire, for reward. He works because he wants money in order that he may enjoy. He works because he wants power in order that the lower self may be gratified. All these activities, these râjasic qualities, are set going with the purpose of ministering to his lower nature. In order that these activities may be trained and regulated to serve the purpose of the Higher Self, he is to be taught to substitute duty for self-gratification, to carry on work as work because it is his duty, to turn the wheel of life because it is his function to turn it, that he may do as Shrî Krishna said He does Himself. He does not act because there is anything for Him to gain either in this world or in any other; but He acts because without His action the world would cease, He acts because without His action the wheel would no longer revolve. And those who accomplish Yoga must act in the spirit of His acting, acting for the whole and not for the separated part, acting for the carrying out of the divine will in the Kosmos and not for the pleasure of the separated entity that imagines itself to be independent when it ought to be a co-worker under Him. This object is to be gained by gradually raising the sphere of these activities. Duty is to be substituted for self-gratification, and religious rites and ceremonies are ordained to train men gradually towards the true life that is their function. Every religious ceremony is but a way of training men into the true and higher life. A man meditates in the early morning and at the going down of the sun, but ultimately his life will be one long meditation. He meditates for an hour to prepare himself for meditating always. All creative activities are the result of meditation, and you will remember that it is by Tapas that all worlds are created. In order then that man may reach that mighty and creative power of meditation, in order that he also may be able to exercise that divine power, he must be trained towards it by religious ceremonies, by intermittent thought, by Tapas taken up and laid down again. Set meditation is a step towards the accomplishment of constant meditation; it takes a part of daily life in order to permeate the whole, and men practice it daily in order that gradually it may absorb the life. The time comes when for the Yogî there is no fixed hour for meditation, for all his life is one long meditation. No matter what outer activities he may be doing he meditates; and he is ever at the Feet of his Lord although both mind and body may be active in the world of man. And so with all other forms of action; first a man learns to perform action as a sacrifice to duty and a paying of his debt to the world in which he is—the paying back to all the different parts of Nature of that which they give to him. And then later, sacrifice becomes more than the paying of a debt; it becomes a joyful giving of everything the man has to give. The partial sacrifice is the debt that is paid, the perfect sacrifice is the gift of the whole. A man gives himself, with all his activities, with all his powers, no longer paying part of his possessions as a debt but all of himself as a gift. And when that stage is reached Yoga is accomplished and the lesson of Karma-Yoga has been learned.

Take as one step towards this those five daily

sacrifices which are familiar in name at least to all of you, and realize what underlay the ordination of those sacrifices. Each one of the five is the payment of a debt, the recognition of what man as a separated individual owes as a debt to the whole around him. And if you consider them for the moment one by one, however hastily, you will see how thoroughly each is this payment of a debt. Take the first: the sacrifice to the Devas. Why is that sacrifice ordained? It is because man has to learn that his body owes a debt to earth and to the Intelligences that guide the processes of Nature by which earth brings forth her fruits, by which she produces nourishment for man; as man takes the nourishment for his body, his body owes back, in payment of the debt, the returning to Nature an equivalent for that which has been given it through the instrumentality of those kosmic Intelligences, those Devas, who guide the forces of the lower world. And so man was taught to pour his sacrifice into the fire. Why? The phrase that was given as an explanation was: "Agni is the mouth of the Gods," and people repeat the phrase and never try to understand its meaning, nor to go below the surface of the external name of the Deva to His function in the world. The real meaning of course that underlies the phrase is that all around on every side there are the conscious and sub-conscious workers in Nature in grade after grade, a great kosmic Deva at the head, as it were, of each division

of that vast army; so that below the Deva as a
Ruler in fire, in air, in water, in earth, below that
particular Deva come a vast number of lower Gods
who carry on the different and separate activities
of the natural forces in the world, the rain, the
productive powers of the earth, the fertilizing
agencies of various sorts. And this first sacrifice
is a feeding of these lower agencies, a giving to
them of food by fire; and fire is called "the mouth
of the Gods" because it disintegrates, because it
changes and transmutes the solid and fluid things
which are placed in it, turns them into vapor, disintegrates them into finer materials, and thus
passes them on into etheric matter to become the
sustenance of those lower grades of elemental lives
that carry out the commands of the kosmic Devas.
And in this way a man pays his debt to them, and
then in return in the lower regions of the atmosphere the rain falls, and the earth produces, and
nourishment is given to man. And that was what
Shrî Krishna meant when he bade man "nourish
the Gods and the Gods shall nourish you." For it
is that lower cycle of nourishment, as it were,
which man has to learn. At first he accepted it as
a religious teaching; then came the period in which
he thought it superstition, knowing not the inner
working and seeing only the outer appearances;
and then comes deeper knowledge when Science,
which tends first to materialism, by deeper study
rises toward recognition of the spiritual realm.

Scientific knowledge begins to say in scientific terms what the Rishis said in terms of the spirit, that man may rule and regulate the working of the lower powers of Nature by action that he himself performs, and in this way growing knowledge justifies the ancient teaching, justifies to the intellect what the spiritual man sees by direct intuition, by the spiritual sight.

Next, there is the sacrifice to the ancestors; the recognition of what man owes to those who went before him in the world, the payment of the debt that he owes to those who worked in the world ere his last coming, the gratitude and veneration which are due to those who partly made the world for us, and brought about improvements that we should inherit them. That service is a debt of gratitude due to those immediately before us in human evolution, who took their part in it during their earthly lives and bequeathed to us the result of their labors. As we reap the benefit of their work, we pay back the debt of gratitude. And so this is one of the daily sacrifices, the recognition of this debt of gratitude to those who have gone before.

And then of course comes the sacrifice of knowledge, that of study, in order that by the study of the sacred words men may be able to help and train those more ignorant than themselves, and may also evolve in themselves the knowledge necessary for the manifestation of the Self within them.

Fourthly, the sacrifice to men, the payment to

some particular man of the duty owed to humanity, the feeding of some particular man as a recognition that men owe to each other all kindly deeds in the physical world, all the assistance that brother can give to brother. The sacrifice to men is the formal recognition of this duty, and in feeding those who are hungry, and in showing hospitality to those who are in need of it, while you feed one man as a concrete fact you feed all humanity ideally and in intention; when you give hospitality to one man who comes past your door, you open the door of your heart to humanity as one great entity, and in helping and sheltering one you give help and shelter to humanity as a whole.

And so also with the last of the five sacrifices, that to animals; food is to be placed on the ground by the householder that any passing animal may take. In this you recognize your duty to the lower world, your duty of giving help, of giving food, of giving training to them. The sacrifice to animals is meant to impress on his mind that we are here as trainers, as directors, as helpers, of the lower creatures that stand beneath us on the ladder of evolution. Every time we sin against them by cruelty, by harshness, by brutality of any sort, we sin against Him who is dwelling within them and whose lower manifestations they also are. And in order that man might recognize the good within the brute, in order that he might understand that Shrî Krishna is in the lower animal, although more veiled than He is in man, man was bidden to sacrifice to the animals, not to the outer form but to the God within. The only way we can sacrifice to them is by kindness, by gentleness, by compassion, by training, by helping forward the animal evolution, and not by beating it back by the brutality and by the cruelty we see around us on every side.

Thus man was taught by these outer rites and ceremonies the inner spiritual truths, by which his life was to be permeated. And when the five sacrifices were over, he was to go out into the world of men still to sacrifice by other forms of action, still to sacrifice by the performance of his daily duties. And his daily life that was begun by these five sacrifices passed out consecrated into the outer life of men. With gradual carelessness as to the five sacrifices has grown carelessness of duty in that outer life of men. Not because these sacrifices in themselves will be for ever necessary, for a time comes when a man rises above them. But remember this: he only rises above them when his whole life has become one long and living sacrifice. Until that is accomplished, these formal recognitions of duty are necessary for the sake of the raising of the life. And unhappily in India today these have largely dropped out of account, not because men have risen above them nor because all their lives are pure, spiritual and lofty, so that they have no need of the lower training and the continual reminder; but because they have become careless and materialistic, and have fallen so far below the ideal of their Manu. They refuse all dutiful recognition to the Powers above them, and therefore they fail in their duty to the men around them.

Let us consider next the outer daily life—the duty of the individual in the world. Wherever it is, he is born into some particular family; that marks his family duties. He is born into some community; that marks out his communal duties. He is born into a particular nation; that marks out his national duties. For each man the limitations of duty are set by the circumstances of his birth, which, under the good Law, under the karmic direction, give to each man the place of his working, the training ground on which he is to learn. Therefore it is said that each man should do his own duty, his own Dharma. Better to do your own, although imperfect, than to try to do the higher Dharma of another. For that into which you are born is that which you need; that into which you are born is your wisest training. Do your own duty careless of results, and then you will learn the lesson of life, and you will begin to tread the path of Yoga. At first of course action will be done for its fruit; men will do it because they desire to gain its reward. And here we understand their early training, where men were taught to work for results in the world of Svarga. The child-man is trained by rewards; Svarga is held out to him as a thing to be gained by work; as he accomplishes his religious rites and duties he ensures their svârgic recompense. And in this way he is induced to practice morality, just as you induce a child to learn its lessons by giving it some reward or some prize. But if action is to be used for Yoga and not for the gaining of reward, either here or in any other world, then it must be done only as duty.

Consider for a moment the four great castes and see how each of these was meant to be used. The Brâhmana was to teach in order that there might be a succession of wise teachers to guide the evolution of the race. He was not to teach for money, he was not to teach for power, he was not to teach for anything he got for himself; he was to teach in fulfillment of his Dharma, and he was to have knowledge that he might in turn hand it on to others. Thus in a well-regulated nation there would be always teachers to instruct, able to guide and advise unselfishly and without a selfish object; thus nothing would be gained by him for himself, but everything would be gained by him for the people. In this way his Dharma would be accomplished and the soul set free.

Then there came the Yoga which was the fitting of the active man of the world for governing and regulating, the training of the dominant class, the Kshattriya. There you had the man who was to rule. Why? Not that he might gratify himself by power, but in order that justice might be done, in order that the poor man might feel secure and the rich man might be unable to tyrannize, in order that fairness and impartial justice might prevail in the struggling world of men. For in the midst of this world of struggle, in the midst of this world of anger and strife, in the midst of this world where men are seeking to gratify the spirit of self instead of the common good, they have to be taught that justice must be done, that if the strong man abuses his strength the just ruler will restrain that unfair exercise of strength, that the weaker shall not be trampled upon, that the weaker shall not be oppressed. And the duty of the king was to do justice between man and man, so that all men might look to the throne as the fountain from which divine justice flowed. That is the ideal of the divine kingship, that is the ideal of the divine ruler. Râma came to teach it, Shrî Krishna came to teach it; but men were so dull that they would not learn the lesson. The Kshattriya used his strength to gratify himself and oppress others, and took their wealth for his own and used their labor for his personal advantage. He lost the ideal of the divine ruler who incarnated justice in the warring world of men. But he was meant to make that ideal the object of his life, and his duty, therefore, was to administer the land, to administer it for the good of the nation and not for the gratification of himself. And so also when his duty was the duty of the soldier. The nation was to carry on its functions in peace. Poor men and harmless men were to live secure with their households round them in happiness and prosperity. The merchant was to carry on the work of a merchant in peace. All the various avocations of life were to be carried on fearlessly, secure against aggression. And so the Kshattriya was taught that when he fought, he was to fight as the defender of the helpless and give his life freely that they might enjoy their lives in peace. He was not to fight because he wanted gain. He was not to fight because he wanted land. He was not to fight because he wanted power or dominion. He was to stand as an iron wall round the nation so that every attack should break itself against his body, and within the circle made by him all men should live in peace, in security and in happiness. If he was to follow Yoga within the duty of the Kshattriya, he must look on himself as the agent of the divine Actor, and therefore it was that Shrî Krishna taught that He had done all and that Arjuna but repeated the action in the world of men. And when the divine Actor is recognized in every action of the man, then he can accomplish action as duty without desire, and it loses its binding power on the soul.

So again with the Vaishya who was to accumulate wealth. He was to do it not for his own gratification, but for the support of the nation. He was to be rich in order that every activity that needed wealth should find a store of wealth at hand and be carried out in every direction. So that everywhere there might be homes for the poor, everywhere rest-houses for the traveller, everywhere hospitals both for men and beasts, everywhere temples for worship, and everywhere the wealth which was needed to support these activities of perfect national life. And so his Dharma was this accumulation for the common good and not for individual self-gratification. In this way he too might follow Yoga, and by Karma-Yoga prepare himself for the higher life.

So also with the Shûdra, who was to perform his Dharma in the commonwealth. His work lay in accomplishing the duty of forming the great hand of the nation, which brought into it what was wanted and carried on the serving external activities. His Yoga, if it were to be accomplished, lay in gladly discharging his duties, doing them for the sake of doing them and not for the reward that by doing them he might gain.

First men do action for self-gratification, in that way experience is gained; then they learn to do it as duty, and so they begin to practise Yoga in their daily life; lastly they do it as a joyful sacrifice for which they ask nothing back, but give every power they possess for the accomplishment of the work. And in this way union is accomplished.

We understand what is meant by purification, when we notice these stages of self-gratification, of doing duty as duty, of giving everything as a free-will sacrifice. These are the stages of the path of purification. But how shall such purification be made as shall lead to the higher steps, to the beginning of the discipleship for which all created activity is to be the preparation? Every part of man must be purified, body as well as mind. On the purification of the body I have not time to dwell, but I may remind you that according to the teaching of the *Bhagavad Gîtâ* it is by way of moderation that this purification is accomplished and not by self-torturing asceticism, torturing the body and Him that dwells within it, as Shrî Krishna says. Yoga is accomplished by temperate self-control, by deliberate training of the lower nature, by quietly choosing the pure path in food, by care and moderation in all physical activities, thus gradually training and regulating and moderating until the whole body comes under the control of the will and of the Self. Therefore the household life was ordained; for men were not fit for the hard road of celibacy, save here and there a few. Brahmacharya was not for all. By household life were men taught to control and moderate their sexual passions, not by crushing them out—which is for the mass of men impossible, and if attempted with unwise energy often results in a re-action that throws the unwise person into the worst profligacy of life—not by single effort which tries to kill and to uproot in a moment, but by gradual training in moderation, and by practising the self-denial of the home, where the lower nature should be slowly trained to temperance and be accustomed to be controlled by the higher, trained out of its over-activity and made utterly subordinate to the One. There is where this Karma-Yoga comes in. The householder has gradually to learn self-control, moderation, making the lower nature yield to the higher, training it day by day until it is absolutely subject to the will. In that way he purifies the body and becomes fitted for the higher paths of Yoga. Then again he must purify the passions of the lower nature all through. Take as an illustration of it—I want to give you three illustrations of this so that you may work it out in your lives—take the passion of anger, and see how it may be worked upon in Karma-Yoga, in order that it may be transmuted in quality. Anger is an energy, an energy that goes out of man to fight his way. You see it in an undeveloped and untrained man as passion, showing itself in many brutal forms, beating down opposition, caring not what methods are used if he strikes out of his way all that which opposes the gratification of his will. And in that form it is an undisciplined and destructive energy of Nature which he who would do Karma-Yoga must most certainly subdue. How shall he subdue and train the passion of anger? He gets rid of the personal element to begin with. When a personal injury is done to him he trains himself to cease to resent it. There is the duty which lies before many of you. Some man does you a wrong; some one does an injustice against you. What shall you do? You may let the passion of anger carry you away and you may strike at him. He has cheated you: you try to injure him in return, and to take advantage of him. He has injured you: you try in turn to injure him. He has gone behind your back: you go behind his back and do him wrong in turn. And so the passion of anger rages, and destruction is seen on every side in what should be the society of men. How shall this passion be purified? You may take the answer from any one of the great Teachers who taught Karma-Yoga, who taught how action in the world of men might be used for the purposes of the Self. You may remember that amongst the ten-fold system of duty which Manu laid down, forgiveness of injuries is one of the duties. You may remember that when the Buddha was teaching He taught "Hatred ceases not by hatred at any time, hatred ceases by love." You may remember that the Christian Teacher followed the same line of thought and He said: "Be not overcome of evil, but overcome evil with good." That is Karma-Yoga. Forgive the injury; give love for hatred; overcome evil with good. In that way you eliminate the personal element; you will no longer feel angry because you are wronged; you will have purified away the personal element, and anger in you will no longer be of this lower kind. But still a form of anger may remain of a higher kind. You see a wrong done to the weak: you are angry with the wrongdoer; you see an animal ill-used: you are wrathful with the person who is cruel; you see a poor man oppressed: you are angry against the oppressor. Impersonal anger—far nobler than the other, and a necessary stage in human evolution; far nobler and better to be angry with a wrongdoer than pass by in stolid indifference, because you have no sympathy with the suffering that is inflicted. That higher, impersonal anger is nobler than indifference, but it is not the highest. It also in turn has to be changed, and it has to be changed into the quality of doing justice to the strong and the weak alike; which compassionates the wrongdoer as well as the wronged; which sees that he injures himself even more than the person whom he hurts; which is sorry for him as well as for the person who suffers under him; which embraces all, wrongdoer and sufferer, in one embrace of love and of justice. The man who has thus purified the passion of anger stops the wrong because it is his duty to stop it, and is gentle to the wrongdoer because he also must be helped and trained; thus what was anger striking back against a personal wrong becomes justice which stops all wrong and makes the strong and the weak equally safe and equally protected. That is the purification which is done in the world of action, that the line of daily effort by which the lower nature is purified in order that union may be attained.

Take again love. You may have that in the lower brutal form—the animal passion between the sexes of the very lowest and the poorest kind, which cares nothing for the character of the one for whom the attachment is felt, which cares nothing for the beauty of the mental and of the moral nature; it cares only for the physical beauty, the physical attraction, and the physical pleasure. There is passion in its lowest form. Self is sought and only self. That is purified by the man who follows Karma-Yoga into love which sacrifices itself for the one who is loved; he performs family duties, he takes care of wife and of child and does his very best for them at the sacrifice of his own inclinations, of his own leisure and his own gratification; he works in order that the family may be better supported, he works in order that the family wants may be supplied; in him love no longer seeks only its own pleasure but seeks to help those who are beloved, and to take on itself the evil that threatens them in order that they may be sheltered and spared and guarded; by following Karma-Yoga the man purifies his love from the selfish elements, and that which was an animal passion for the other sex becomes the love of the husband, of the father, of the elder brother, of the relative, who fulfils his duty, working for the sake of the loved and in order that their lives may be fairer and happier. And then there comes the last stage, when the love that is purified from self goes out to all. Not only in the narrow circle of the home does it work, but it sees in every one whom it meets a person who is to be helped, sees a brother to be fed in every starving man, sees a sister to be protected in every woman who is left forlorn. Finding anyone who is lonely, a man thus purified becomes father and brother and helper to that one, not because he loves personally but because he loves ideally, and because he seeks to give for love's sake and not even for the gratification of being loved in return. The highest love, the love that grows out of Karma-Yoga, asks nothing back in return for what it gives; it seeks no gratitude; it asks for no recognition; it is willing to work unknown; nay, it is more glad to work unknown and unrecognized than to work in a way that brings recognition and that brings praise. And the ultimate purification of love is where that love becomes absolutely divine, where it gives because it is its nature to spread happiness, where it asks nothing for itself but seeks only that others should be glad.

And so again with greed, covetousness. Men seek to gain in order that they may enjoy; they desire gain in order that they may have power; they strive to gain in order that they may be lifted up. They purify that first form of greed; and they begin to desire gain that the family may be better off, that the family may be in a better position, that the family may be beyond suffering and want and starvation; thus they grow less selfish than before. Then they go further. They desire power in order that they may use it for good, that they may spread it to do good over a wider area than the family, that they may serve in a wider field than the home; and at last, as in the case of love, they learn to give without any return. They learn to desire knowledge and power not that they may hold it but that they may give it, not that they may enjoy it but only in order that it may be spread. And in this way selfishness is burned up.

Have you ever wondered why He to whom is given the name of Mahâdeva, why He dwells in a burning-ground? A strange place, men would have thought, in which the Mightiest One should dwell. Strange surroundings with which to environ Him who is purity itself. What is hidden under the symbolism of the burning-ground is human life; and in that burning-ground where Shiva dwells all the lower things in human life are consumed as by fire. If He dwells not within it, then these earthly things remain to putrefy, to corrupt, to be a source of danger, to spread disease and corruption everywhere. But in the burning-ground in which He dwells, through which His fire passes from side to side, is burned up everything that is selfish, everything that is personal, everything which is of the lower nature; out of those regenerating flames the Yogî rises triumphant, with noth-

ing of the personal element left within him; for
the fire of the Lord has burned up all lower passions, and there is nothing there remaining to corrupt or to spread disease. Therefore is He called
the Destroyer—the Destroyer of the lower in order
that regeneration may come; for out of His Fire
the soul was originally born, and from that burning-ground the purified Self arises.

Thus do these first steps lead onward towards
true discipleship, lead onward towards the finding
of the Guru, lead onward towards the Inner Temple, the holiest of holies, where the Guru of humanity resides. These are the first steps that you
must take, this is the route by which you must
travel. Men you are, living in the world and
bound by worldly ties, men living the social and
political life; and yet at the back of your hearts
you are desiring true Yoga and the knowledge
which is of the permanent and not only of the
transitory life. For in the hearts of every one of
you, if you go down to the very bottom of them,
you will find a yearning to know something more,
a desire to live more nobly than you live today. You
may have the outer appearance of loving the things
of the world, and you do love them with your lower natures; but in the heart of every true Hindu,
who is not absolutely renegade and apostate to his
religion and his country, there is still an inner
yearning for something more than the things of
earth, still a faint longing, if only from the past

traditions, that India shall be nobler than she is today and her people more worthy of her past. Here then is the route that you must begin to tread: no great nation unless individuals are great; no mighty people if individuals are sordid and poor and selfish in their lives. You must begin where you are today, in the life that you are leading; and following these lines that I have roughly sketched you will take your first steps towards the Path.

Let me close by reminding you of what the end of that Path is, although I have still to take you further towards it in the lectures that lie before us in these morning hours. The end of the Path is union—the Karma-Yoga which we have been studying is Union by Action. There are other steps to take, but what is "union"? You remember how Shrî Krishna gave the marks of the man who had passed beyond the gunas, the marks of the man who had crossed beyond them and who was fit for the nectar of immortality, the man who was ready to know that which is Highest, to come into union with the Supreme. He perceives no agent save the gunas. He knows That which lies beyond. He sees the gunas acting; he desires them not when they are absent, he repels them not when they are present. He is balanced amidst friends and foes, balanced in praise and in shame, self-reliant, looking on all things with an equal eye, on the clod of earth, on the piece of gold, on friend and on enemy alike. He is the same to all, for he has crossed over the gunas, and is no longer deluded by their play. That is the goal that we are seeking. These are the first steps towards the Path that crosses over. Until these are trodden no other steps are possible; but as these are gradually accomplished the beginning of the true Path is seen.

## QUALIFICATIONS FOR DISCIPLESHIP

CONTROL OF MIND.    MEDITATION.    BUILDING OF
CHARACTER

BROTHERS,—The special section of the subject with which I am to deal this morning is the qualifications for discipleship. And let me begin by drawing your attention to the question of re-birth, and the way in which a man may realize what is meant by discipleship, and may deliberately choose that as his future path in life. You will remember what was said yesterday, how I traced for you the different stages of action: how a man first performed action for the gratification of his own lower nature ever seeking for fruit, how then he gradually learnt in the practice of Karma-Yoga to perform action not for the sake of the fruit for the lower self, but because the action ought to be done, thus identifying himself with Law, thus consciously taking part in the great work of the world. Then I hinted to you that there was a stage beyond that where the sacrifice was made not only as duty but as a joyful giving of everything that a man possessed. It is clear that when that stage is aimed at, when a man performs work not merely because it ought to be done but because he desires to give everything that he is and has to the service of the Supreme, then it is that it becomes possible for a man to break what are called the bonds of desire and in that way to liberate himself from re-birth. For that which draws man to re-birth in the world is desire; the desire to enjoy the things that here may be enjoyed, the desire to achieve the things that here may be achieved. Every man who puts before him some earthly aim, every man who makes the goal of his life some earthly object, that man is evidently bound by desire. And so long as he desires that which the earth can give him, he must return for it; so long as any joy or any object belonging to the transitory life—physical life upon earth—is a thing that has power to attract, it is a thing that has also power to bind. Every attraction in other words is that which binds the soul, and brings it back to the place where the desire may be accomplished.

Man is so divine in his nature, so God-like in himself, that even this out-going energy of his, that we speak of as desire, has in itself the power of accomplishment. That which he desires he attains, that which he desires nature gives to him in due course when the time is ripe; so that man, as has often been said, is master of his own destiny, and whatever he demands from the universe that the universe will give. He must of course take the results of the desire in that portion of the universe to which the desire belongs. So that if he desires the things of the earth, he must come back to earth in order that the desire may be accomplished. So again a man is bound to re-birth by any of those desires which find their satisfaction in the temporary and transitory worlds on the other side of death; those worlds which are transitory, beyond the gate-way of death, all lead back again, as we know, to re-birth here; so that if a man's desires are fixed on the joys of Svarga, if he looks for the fruits of his life in this world in some other world which is also transitory, supposing that he denies himself earthly joys with the deliberate object of attaining the joys of Svarga, then those joys are the fruit of his work, and that fruit will be given to him in due course. But inasmuch as Svarga is itself fleeting, inasmuch as Svarga is itself transitory, he has only taken for his path what has been called the path of the Moon, the path that leads to re-birth—you may remember it is written that "the moon is the door of Svarga"—and then from Svarga the soul comes back to the earthly world of men. In that way desire—whether it is to be accomplished in this world or in some other world, also transitory and fleeting—ties the soul to re-birth, and therefore it is that it is written that only when "the bonds of the heart are broken" can the soul reach liberation.

Now liberation pure and simple (for an age) may be gained by this mere destruction of desire.

Without any very high achievement, without any very lofty stage in the evolution of the soul, without the unfolding of all the divine possibilities that lie enwrapped in human consciousness, without attaining those great heights on which the Teachers and the Helpers of mankind are standing, man may gain, if he so desire it, a liberation which is fundamentally selfish, which lifts him indeed out of the world of change, which breaks indeed the bonds that bind him to the worlds of life and death, but which helps not in any way his brethren, which does not break their bonds nor set them free; this is a liberation which is for the unit rather than for the whole, in which a man passes out of humanity and leaves humanity to struggle along its way. I know that many men have in life no higher thought than that; that there are many who seek simply for liberation, careless of others so that they themselves escape. That, as I say, may fairly easily be gained. It needs a recognition of the transitoriness of earthly things, of the worthlessness of the objects of ambition with which a worldly man naturally busies himself day by day. But after all that liberation is only for a time, for a manvantara perhaps; after that there is a return. So that while it sets the soul free from this world and leaves it liberated so far as this earth is concerned, in a future cycle such souls have to come back to take another step towards what is the really diviner destiny of man, the evolution of the human conscious-

ness into the All-consciousness which is to be used
for training, for helping, for guiding the worlds
of the future.

I turn aside then from that to those wiser and
more generous souls who while they would break
the bonds of desire would fain break them not that
they themselves may escape from the difficulties
of earthly life, but in order that they may follow
that higher and nobler Path which is called the
Path of Discipleship, follow the Great Ones who
have made the pathway possible for humanity;
such seek to discover the Teachers who are willing
to accept those who qualify themselves for discipleship with a view not of simply liberating themselves, not of simply gaining escape from trouble,
but of becoming the helpers and teachers and saviours of humanity, giving back to the world at
large that which the individual has received from
the Teachers who have gone in front. That discipleship is hinted at in all the great Scriptures of
the world. The Guru who may be found and who
teaches men is one of the ideals of all the highest
and most developed souls who in this outer world
have sought to realize the divine. Take any Scripture that you will, and see how this thought is ex-
pressed there. Take Upanishad after Upanishad
and see how the Guru is mentioned and how the
attention of the would-be disciple is directed towards His seeking and His finding. It is that
which I desire to put to you this morning; the qual-

ifications for discipleship; that which has to be done before discipleship is possible; that which has to be accomplished before the search for the Guru has any chance of success; that which has to be done in the world, in the ordinary life of men, utilizing that life as a school, as a place for learning the preparatory lessons, as a place for qualifying the man to be fit to touch the Feet of the Great Teachers who shall give him the true re-birth—the re-birth which is symbolized in all exoteric religions by one or another external ceremony, sacred less for itself than because of that which it symbolizes. You will find in Hinduism the word "Twice-born," implying that the man is not only born of earthly father and mother, but has passed the true second birth which is given by the Guru to the soul. That is symbolized—alas! only symbolized, in too many cases now—by the initiation given by the family Guru or by the father to the son, when he becomes what in the outer world is called the twice-born man. But in the days of old —and in the present days as well—there was and is a real, a true Initiation which is the original of that external ceremony; there is a real, a true Initiation which is not simply initiation into an exoteric caste but into a really divine birth; which is given by a mighty GURU; which comes from the GREAT INITIATOR, the One Initiator of humanity. We read of these initiations in the past, we know them to exist in the present. All history bears testimony to their reality. There are temples in India beneath which are the places of the ancient initiations, places which now are unknown to the people, places which now are hidden from the eyes of men, but which none the less are there, which none the less are accessible to those who prove themselves worthy to attain them. And not in India alone are such places to be found. Ancient Egypt had also her crypts of initiation, and mighty pyramids in one or two cases stand over the ancient places, that now are hidden from the eyes of man. The latter initiations that took place in Egypt, those of which you may read in the history of Greece and the history of Egypt itself, those of which you may have heard that one or another of the great philosophers was there initiated—those took place in the outer buildings known to the people, which covered the real Temples of Initiation. Into these entrance was not gained by outer knowledge, but under conditions that have existed from the furthest antiquity and that exist today as really as they existed then; for as all history bears testimony to the reality of the initiation, so does history bear testimony to the reality of the Initiate. There stand at the head of every great religion Men who were more than ordinary men, Men who gave the Scriptures to the people, Men who traced the outlines of the exoteric faiths, Men who stand out in history head and shoulders above Their fellows by the spiritual wisdom that gave Them glory and the spiritual insight by means of which They saw, and who testified of what They saw; for there has been one note which we have often remarked with regard to all these great Teachers. They do not argue, They proclaim; They do not discuss, They declare; They do not reach Their conclusions by logical processes, They reach them by spiritual intuitions; They come forth and speak with authority that justifies itself in the very speaking, and men's hearts recognize the truth of Their teaching, even when it rises higher than their intellect is able to follow. For there is in the heart of every man that spiritual principle to which every divine Teacher makes His appeal, and it answers to the truth of the spiritual declaration, even though the intellectual eyes may not be keen enough to discern the reality of that which the Spirit sees. Those great Gurus then who are found in history as the greatest Teachers, as well as Those whom we find standing out as the mightiest philosophers. Those are the Initiates, who have become more than man; such Initiates exist today as they have ever existed. Nay, how should death touch Them who have overcome life and death, and are the Masters of all lower nature? They have evolved out of humanity in the course of the millennia which lie behind, some out of our humanity and some out of humanities anterior to our own. Some of Them came from other worlds, from other planets, when our humanity was a child; others grew up when this humanity had trodden long enough the path of evolution to produce its own Initiates, Gurus of our own race to help onwards the humanity to which They Themselves belong. When that path is trodden and that goal is reached, for such a Man there is no more possibility that death should have power over Him, and that having been He shall not continue to be; the very fact that they are found in history is the guarantee for Their present existence; that would be enough to show that They exist, without the testimony which is growing year by year of those who have found Them, and who know Them, those who are taught by Them, who take lessons at Their Feet. For in our own time and in our own day, one after another finds the ancient path; in our own time and our own day one after another finds that ancient and narrow path, keen as the edge of a razor, that leads onward to the gateway of discipleship and makes entrance on the Path of Discipleship a possibility for men; as one after another finds it, one witness after another in modern times is able to proclaim the truth of the ancient writings, and entering on that Path they may follow it stage by stage.

But for the moment we are concerned with finding what qualifications are demanded ere entrance to the Path may be gained. Now the first of these qualifications is one which must be met to a very considerable extent at least before discipleship in any sense is possible. One of these qualifications is what is called control of the mind, and my first task now is to explain to you very definitely what control of the mind means, what the mind is which is controlled, and who it is that controls it. For you must remember that for the great mass of people the mind is the representative of the man. When he speaks of "himself," he really means his mind. When he says "I," he is identifying that "I" with the mind, the conscious intelligence that knows; and when he says "I think, I feel, I know," you will not find, if you inquire closely into the meaning, that he goes beyond the limits of his consciousness in his waking hours. That is what he means by the "I," for the most part. Certainly those who have studied carefully know that such an "I" is illusory; but while they know it as an intellectual proposition, they do not realize it as a practical matter in life. They may admit it as philosophers, they do not live it as men in the world. And in order that we may understand clearly what this control of mind is, and how we may control the mind, let us just for a moment pause at what we call self-control when we are dealing with the man of the world; and we shall see how very inadequate that is when it is compared with the self-control which is one of the qualifications for discipleship. When we say a man is self-controlled we mean that his mind is stronger than his passions; that if you take the lower nature, the passions and the emotions, and

over against that you set the intellectual nature,
the mind and the will and the reasoning power and
the judgment, that these last are stronger than the
first; that the man is able in a moment of temptation, under an appeal to his passions, to say: ''No,
I will not yield to that; I will not permit myself to
be carried away by passion, I will not allow myself
to be run away with by means of the senses; these
senses are simply the horses that draw my chariot;
I am the driver, and I will not permit them to gallop
along the road they desire''; and then we say that
that man is self-controlled. That is the ordinary
sense of the word, and mind you, that self-control
is an admirable quality. It is a stage through
which every man must pass. The uncontrolled and
unregulated man, who is subject entirely to the
senses, he indeed has much to do ere even this
quality of worldly self-control will be acquired;
but very very much more than that is wanted.
When we talk about a strong-willed man and a weak
man, we mean for the most part that the man who
has got a strong will is a man who under the ordinary circumstances of temptation and difficulty
will choose his path by reason and by judgment,
and will guide himself by the memory of the past
and by conclusions which are based thereon; then
we say a man has a strong will; he is not a man
who is at the mercy of circumstances; he is not
a prey to every impulse, he is not like a ship carried by the currents of the river or driven about

by the winds as they blow upon it. He is rather
like a ship controlled by a seaman who understands his duty, who utilizes the currents and the
winds to drive his ship in the direction in which
he desires to go, who uses the rudder of the will to
make the ship follow the path on which he himself
has determined. And it is true that this difference
of strong and of weak will is a mark of growing individuality; as the man himself grows, as the individuality increases, this power of direction from
within is one of the clearest marks of the growth.
I remember H. P. Blavatsky saying in one of her
articles when she was dealing with individuality,
that you might recognize individuality in man and
the absence of individuality in the lower animals
by observing the way in which the man and the
lower animals act under certain circumstances. If
you take a number of wild animals and surround
them with similar circumstances, you will find
they all act in the same general way. Their action
is determined by the circumstances that surround
them; each does not arrange his own action to mod-
ify the circumstances, balancing the one against
the other in order to make the path which he se-
lects; they act all alike. If you know the nature
of the animal, and if you know the circumstances,
you might judge of the action of the whole class
by the actions of one or two. Now that distinctly
shows the absence of individuality. But if you
take men, a number of men, you cannot judge be-

forehand that they will all act in the same way; for according to the development of the individuals will be the variety of the action taken by them under the same circumstances. One individual is different from another, therefore he acts differently; he has a will of his own, therefore he chooses differently, the man who is weak-willed has less individuality, he is less developed, he is not as far advanced on the road of evolution.

Now supposing that this is realized, then a man may go a step further than the control of the lower nature by the higher, and he may begin to realize something of the creative power of thought. This will imply more than the thought of the ordinary man of the world; it will imply knowledge of some philosophy. If for instance he has studied the great writings of the Hindus he will there gain a definite intellectual apprehension of the creative power of thought, but the moment he has seen that he will further see that there is something behind what he calls his mind; for if there be a creative power of thought, if a man can generate thought through the mind, then there must be something that generates, and that is hidden behind the mind producing these thoughts. The very fact that there is such a creative power of thought, that a man is able to influence and train his own mind and the mind of others by this creative power is enough to show that there is something behind the mind, something which is as it were separable from it, and something that will use the mind as its instrument. And then there dawns on the student who is endeavoring to understand himself, that he has to deal with a mind which is exceedingly difficult to deal with, and that thoughts come unbidden, and spring up as it were without choice of his own; when he begins to study the workings of the mind he finds thoughts come rushing into it without his asking them to come; he finds himself possessed of ideas which he would wish very different. All kinds of fancies come into his mind which he wants to expel; he finds himself helpless, he cannot get rid of them. He finds himself compelled to grind on at thoughts that dominate the mind and which are by no means at his bidding nor under his authority. And he begins to observe these thoughts; he begins to ask: whence come they? how do they work? how may they be controlled? and he gradually learns that many thoughts that come to his mind have their origin in the minds of other men, and that according to the line of his own thinking so will he attract from the outer world of thought the thoughts of others; in turn he influences the minds of others by the thoughts that are generated by himself, and he begins to understand that this responsibility is much greater than he ever dreamed. He used to think that only when he spoke did he affect the minds of others, only when he acted did he by example influence the actions of others; but as he learns more and more he begins to understand that there is an invisible power which goes out from the thinking man and plays on the minds of other people. Modern science tells us something of this, and to the same effect; modern science in many of its experiments has learned that thought may be sent from brain to brain without the spoken word or without the written message, and that there is something in thought which is palpable, which is observable, which is like a vibration that sets other things vibrating, although no word be formulated, no articulate speech be uttered. Science has discovered that in silence thought may be sent from man to man, that without any outer communication—or as Professor Lodge said, without material means of communication, using the word "material" in its physical sense—it is possible for mind to affect mind.

If that be so, we are all affecting each other by thought without either word or action; for the thought that we have generated goes out into the world to affect the minds of other men; the thoughts that they think come to us to affect in turn our thinking, and we begin to realize that for the most part thinking is a very small part of the life of most people, and that the mere receiving of other people's thoughts is what we are apt to call thinking. In fact men's minds are very much like houses, rest-houses, through which travellers pass and in which they stay for a night; most men's minds are not very much more than that. The thought comes in and goes out. The man contributes very little towards the thought he receives. He receives it, harbors it, and it passes away. But what we ought to be doing is to be thinking deliberately, and thinking with a purpose behind the thought to accomplish that which we determine.

Why should this control of mind, this control of thought, this stopping of thought, this refusing of harborage to the thoughts of others, be so valuable? Why should this be a condition of discipleship? Because when a man becomes a disciple his thoughts gain added power; because when a man becomes a disciple his individuality is growing, is increasing, is becoming mightier; and every thought that he thinks has increased vitality and increased energy and influence on the outer world of man. By a thought a man can kill; by a thought a man can heal a disease; by a thought a man can influence a crowd; by a thought a man can create a visible illusion which shall deceive other men and lead them astray. As thought has such mighty power as the individual grows and increases, and as discipleship means the rapid growth and the increase of individuality, so that a man accomplishes in a few lives what otherwise would take millennia of years to accomplish, it is necessary, before these added powers come within his reach, that he should learn to control his thoughts, that he should learn to check all that is evil in them, that he should learn to harbor nothing save that

which is pure and beneficent and useful. Control
then of the mind by the Self is made a condition
of discipleship, because ere a man has the added
power of thought that comes from the teaching of
the Guru, he must have obtained control over the
instrument by which the thoughts are produced,
so that it may make what he determines that it
shall make, and produce nothing without his full
consent.

I know that on this point people will feel difficulty. They will say: what is this individual that
is always growing? What is this individual who
develops will and power of control over the mind,
who, you say, is not the mind but is greater than
the mind? May I take a picture from the outer
world so as to help you to image in your thinking
the way in which the individual comes to be and
the way in which he grows? Suppose that you
went into an atmosphere supercharged with watery
vapor, but the atmosphere was so hot that the
water remained in suspension, invisible, so that the
place seemed to you to be empty; nothing is there,
you would say, it is empty air. You know quite
well that if a chemist took some of that air thus
charged with vapor, enclosed it, and gradually
cooled it down, you would see appear out of the
emptiness a faint mist or cloudiness, and that faint
mist would gradually grow a little denser and a
little denser, until, as more and more the atmosphere was chilled, there would be formed a drop

of water where before nothing was seen. Now that may serve as one of the clumsy physical images that one may take to illustrate the formation of the individual. Out of that Invisible which is the One from which all proceeds, appears as it were a faint cloud becoming visible, a faint mist condensing, which separates itself from the invisible vapor around it, and gradually condenses more and more till it becomes the individual drop, that we recognize as a unit; out of that which is All comes the separated and distinct; one indeed in its nature with the All, the same in its essence but separated by its conditions, and so individualized out of the whole. And the individual soul of man is such an individualization from the One Self, and it grows and grows by experience. It grows and increases and develops as it is re-born life after life and time after time, hundreds of times into the world. And what we call the mind is just a little out-putting of this individual into the world of matter. As the amœba when it wants food thrusts out a portion of itself and takes in a little particle of nutritive matter and draws the protruded part containing the food back into its own substance, thus nourishing itself with the food that it takes in, so does the individual put out into the world— the physical world—a little protrusion from itself, to gather experience as food for the individual, and draw it in again in what we call death, absorbing this gained experience to nourish its growth.

And the mind is this out-putting into the physical world, it is part of the individual, of the soul; the consciousness that is you is greater than that which you recognize as the intellect. All your past, all the experience that you have gained, is garnered in consciousness. All the knowledge that you have acquired is treasured in the consciousness that is really you. You put out at your birth a little part of yourself to gather new experience and to increase this consciousness still more; this the soul takes for its own growth, and in each life out of its wider consciousness it tries to influence that output portion of itself; what we call the voice of conscience is nothing but this greater Self speaking to the lower self, and trying to guide the lower self in its ignorance by the wisdom which the Higher-Self has acquired life after life.

But we know there is a difficulty about this lower self of ours, the mind. Do you remember what Arjuna said to Shrî Krishna when he was dealing with this control of the lower Manas that we are studying? You remember how he said to his divine Teacher that Manas was so restless; "Manas is verily restless," he said, "O Krishna; it is impetuous, strong, and difficult to bend; I deem it as hard to curb as the wind." And that is true; every one knows it to be true who tries to curb the mind. Every one who tries to control Manas knows how restless, impetuous, and strong it is, and how hard to curb. But do you remember how the

Blessed Lord gave answer to Arjuna when he said it was hard as the wind to curb? His answer was: "Without doubt Manas is hard to curb and restless, O mighty-armed; but it may be curbed by constant practice and by indifference." There is no other way. Constant practice: no one can do it for you; no Teacher can accomplish it for you. You yourselves must do it, and until you begin to take it in hand no finding of the Guru is possible for you. It is useless to cry out and desire to find, if you will not take the steps that are laid down in the published words of all the great Teachers in order to guide you to Their Feet. Here is a mighty Teacher, an Avatâra, who lays down what must be done and who says it may be done. And when an Avatâra says it may be done, He means that it can be done by the man who wills it; for He knows the powers of those whom He can see, and whom He as the Supreme has brought into the world; and when He gives His divine word that the conquest is possible, shall we dare to say that we cannot do it, and so as it were give the lie to God that speaks?

How then shall it be done? "By constant practice," says the Lord; that is to say in your daily life as you have it, in the busy life of men, you are to begin to train this restless mind of yours and make it subject to your will. Try for a moment to think steadily. You will find your thoughts fly away. What shall you do? bring them back again to the point on which you desire to fix them. Choose a subject and then think definitely and consecutively upon it. Remember you have an immense advantage in this training of the mind: you have the ancient Hindu traditions, you have the physical heredity which has been moulded under these conditions, and the training in your youth which ought to have accustomed you to this regulation of the mind. It is far harder for a western-born person to conquer the restlessness of the mind than it ought to be for you, because there the control of mind has not been taught, there the training of the mind is not part of the religious education in the same way, and men are inclined to fly from one subject to another. The habit—to take a trivial case—of constant newspaper reading, three or four papers, perhaps, a day, is one of the things that makes very difficult the control of the mind. You fly from one subject to another; here a number of telegrams that whirl the mind off to England, to France, to Spain, to Kamskatcha, to New Zealand, to America; when you have read that column or half-column you find another kind of news. Accounts of the doings of well-known people. Reports of plays in the theaters, of cases in the lawcourts. Here a race of ships or of men; there descriptions of sports or athletics, and so on. You all know the varied contents of the newspaper. Men do not understand the harm they do themselves by wasting the energies of the mind as they habitually waste them on these trivial and unimportant matters. You will find men in England, I know, who will read half a dozen papers every day; that means more than that they are for the time scattering the power of the mind; for if you scatter them day after day you get into the habit of scattering, and you cannot then readily concentrate your thoughts on one idea. In addition to that there is the waste of time which might be given to higher matters. I do not mean to say that as men in the world you should not know what is going on in the world around you; but it is quite enough to take up a single paper which deals with the more important matters of the outer world, and read quietly through for a few minutes; if you know how to read, that is enough so far as these outside things go.

In order that you may fight against this modern tendency of scattering thought you should make it a daily habit to think consecutively and to concentrate your attention for some time on one subject; make it a serious practice in the training of your mind to read every day some part of a book that deals with the graver matters of life, with the eternal rather than with the transitory; fix the mind upon it while you are reading. Do not allow it to wander, do not allow it to scatter. If it travels off bring it back, and place it again on the same idea, and in that way you will strengthen the mind, you will begin to curb it, you will by constant practice learn to control it, and make it go along the path that you desire it should follow. Even in things of the world this quality is of great advantage. It is not only that in doing this you are preparing yourself for the greater life which is open to you, but even in the common things of life the man of concentrated thought is the more successful man; the man who is able to think consecutively, clearly and definitely, he is the man who even in the lower world will be able to make his way. So you will find this constant practice in training the mind useful in this unimportant world as well as in greater things. And then you will gradually learn the control which is one of the conditions of discipleship.

As you thus train the mind you will perhaps take another step—meditation. Meditation is the deliberate and formal training of the mind in concentration and in fixity of thought. You are to do it every day, because if you do it every day you are helped by what is called the automatism of the body and mind. That which you do daily becomes a habit; that which is done daily is done without an effort after a time; that which is hard to begin with becomes easy by practice. Now meditation may be taken partly as devotional and partly as intellectual, and the wise man who is training himself for discipleship will meditate in both ways. He will concentrate his mind, fix his thought, on the divine ideal, on the Teacher whom, unknown at present, he still ultimately hopes to find; and keeping before him this perfect ideal, he will fix his lower mind on that ideal in the hour of meditation, and will aspire upwards towards it with fixed and unswerving thought. As the mind grows, this will become easier and easier; as he keeps this ideal before the mind in meditation he will begin to reflect it, to grow a little like it. That is one of the creative powers of the mind—the man becomes that upon which he reflects; and if he reflects daily on the perfect ideal of humanity he will begin to grow towards that perfect ideal himself. Then he will gradually find that as he fixes the mind steadily on this ideal, as he aspires upwards towards it, and longs to come into contact with it, he will find during this time of meditation that the lower mind will become peaceful, that the lower mind will sink into quietude, that the outside world will fade away from consciousness, and that the deeper consciousness will shine as it were from within—the higher consciousness, that of the individual himself, realizing and knowing what he is. For as the lower mind is thus quieted, as its restlessness is conquered, it becomes like a still lake of water which is unruffled by any wind, unmoved by any currents. That lake is like a mirror; on that mirror-like surface, unruffled, tranquil, the sun which is in heaven shines down, reflecting itself in the quiet water; so also the higher consciousness reflects itself in the mirror of the tranquillized lower mind. And then the man knows, no longer by authority but of his own knowledge, that he is more than the mind which he has realized as intellect, that his consciousness is greater than the passing consciousness of the mind; then it becomes possible for him to begin to identify himself with the higher, and if only for a moment to catch a glimpse of the majesty of the Self. For remember how in the great Scriptures you are always taught that you yourself are the higher and not the lower. What means the saying that we read in the *Chhândogyopanishad* and elsewhere, the proclamation: "Thou art Brahman," "Thou art That"? so the Buddhists repeat also: "Thou art Buddha." That will never be a *fact* of consciousness to you, however much you may intellectually realize it, until by meditation you have made the lower mind the mirror in which the higher may be reflected; then, in a further stage of meditation you yourself will consciously become the higher, and then you will know what every great Teacher has meant by that famous phrase, which has in it the assertion of the inherent divinity of man.

When this is done daily, is practiced by meditation followed day after day, month after month, year after year, it gradually permeates all the life and becomes constant instead of partial. First, confined to the time of meditation; then spreading over into the life led in the world. You may say:

How can I be conscious of that when I am busy in the outer world? How can I keep consciousness of the higher when the lower is in full activity? Do you not know how, bowing before the altar, you may use your body to offer flowers, whilst the mind is concentrated on the Deity Himself? The outer activity of the body is there, yet your thought is not on the flowers that you are offering but on the Object of the offering; the hands perform their duty and offer their flowers perfectly, although the mind is fixing its thoughts on the Divine itself. And so in the outer world of man, you may offer the flowers of duty in a life of constant activities, of daily work; you may offer these flowers with the body and with the mind, fulfilling to the utmost your duty in the outer world, but you yourselves will be fixed ever in meditation and in worship. Once learn to separate your higher consciousness from your lower, yourself from your mind, and you will gradually acquire the power of carrying on mental activities without losing the real "I" in them, the mind working perfectly at its appropriate duties while the Self remains at a loftier height. You will never leave the inner sanctuary, however much the outer life is busy in the world of men. In this way the man is preparing himself for discipleship.

There is another stage which we must just glance at, that which I call the intellectual side of meditation, concerned with the gradual and

conscious building of character. Again I turn to
the great treatise of Karma-Yoga, the teachings of
Shrî-Krishna in the *Bhagavad Gîtâ*. If you turn
to the 16th discourse you may find the long list
of qualities there given which a man must develop
in himself so that he may be born with them in
the future. They are called "the divine properties," and Arjuna is told: "Thou art born with
divine properties, O Pândava." Now in order that
you may be born with them in future births you
must make them in the birth that is; if you are
to bring them back with you into life you must
gradually create them in lives as they come one
after another, and the man of the world who wants
to know how to build his character can do nothing
better than take this list of qualities, the divine
properties which are wanted in discipleship, and
build them one by one in his daily life by a con-
joint process of meditation and action. Purity for
instance is one of them. How shall a man build
himself into purity? By, in his morning meditation, taking purity as part of the subject on which
he thinks, realizing what it means. No impurity
of thought must ever touch him; no impurity of
action must ever stain him, he must be pure in
the threefold thread of action, word and thought.
That is the threefold cord of duty, as I once reminded you, and is that which the Brâhmana's
threefold thread is intended to represent. In the
morning he thinks of purity as a thing that is

desirable, that he must accomplish; and when he goes out into the world he carries the memory of his meditation with him. He watches his actions; he allows no impure action to stain his body; he commits no impure action all through the day, for he steadily watches every action that no touch of impurity may soil it. He watches his words. He speaks no word that is impure; he makes no reference in his talk to an unclean subject; he never permits his tongue to be soiled by making an unclean suggestion. Every word of his is pure, so that he would dare to speak it in the presence of his Master, whose eye sees every lightest stain of impurity which the ordinary mortal eye would miss. He will watch every word that it may be the purest that he can utter, and he will never foul himself or others by a single word or phrase coarse with impure suggestion. His thought will be pure. He will never allow an unclean thought to come into his mind, or if it comes into his mind it will at once be cast out; the moment the thought comes he will cast it out; and as he knows that it could not come into his mind unless there was in his mind something to attract it, he purifies his own mind, so that no unclean thought of any one else may be able to gain entrance. Thus he watches on this one point through the whole of his day. And then again he will take truth in his morning meditation; he will think of truth, its value in the world, its value in society, its value in his own character; and when he goes out into the world of men he will never commit an action that will give a false impression, he will never speak a word that conveys a false idea. Not only will he not lie, but he will not even be inaccurate, because that also is speaking a falsehood. To be inaccurate in recounting what you have seen is to speak untruth. All exaggeration and painting up of a story, everything that is not perfectly consistent with fact, so far as he knows it, everything which has any shade of untruthfulness, may not be used by him who would become a disciple. And so in thought again he must be true. Every thought must be as true as he can make it, with no shadow of falsehood to pollute his mind. So with compassion. He will meditate on compassion in the morning and during the day he will seek to practice it; he will show all kindness to people around him; he will do all service to family and friends and neighbors. Wherever he sees want he will try to relieve it; wherever he sees sorrow he will try to comfort it; wherever he sees misery he will strive to lighten it. He will live compassion as well as think it, and so make it part of his character. So with fortitude. He will think of the nobility of the strong man, the man whom no outer circumstances can depress or elate, the man who is not joyful over success nor miserable over failure, who is not at the mercy of circumstances, sad today because things are troublesome and joyful to-morrow because things are easy. He will try to be himself, always balanced and strong; as he goes out into the world he will practice; if trouble comes, he will think of the Eternal where no trouble is; if loss of money comes, he will think of the wealth of wisdom that cannot be taken away from him; if a friend be snatched by death, he will consider that no living soul can die and that the body that dies is only the garment which is thrown aside when it is out-worn, and another taken, and that his friend shall be found again. And so with all the other virtues of self-restraint, of peaceableness, of fearlessness—all these things he will think of and practice. Not all at once. No man living in the world would be able to give sufficient time to meditate on each of these every day; but take them one by one, and build them into your character. Work on steadily: do not be afraid of giving time to it; do not be afraid of giving trouble to it. Everything that you build you are building for eternity, and you may well be patient in time when eternity spreads before you. Everything you gain, you gain for evermore. Meditation alone or practice alone is insufficient for the building of a character. Both must go together; both must form part of the daily life, and in this way a noble character is made.

A man who has thus trained himself, a man who has thus done the utmost that he can do, who has given his time and thought and trouble to make himself fit to find the Teacher, even by him the Teacher shall verily be found; or rather, the Teacher shall find him and manifest Himself to his soul. For do you imagine in blindness and in ignorance that these Teachers desire to be hidden? Do you imagine, veiled in illusion, that They deliberately hide Themselves from the eyes of men in order to leave humanity to stumble helpless, unwishful to aid it and to guide? I tell you that much as you may for a moment desire to find your Teacher, the Teacher is a thousandfold more constant in His desire to find you, in order that He may help. Looking out over the world of men, They see so many helpers are wanted and so few are found. The masses perish in ignorance; Teachers are wanted for them and they perish by myriads; there is none to help them. The great Teachers need disciples who are living in the lower world, and who, trained by the Teachers, shall go out into the world of men, and bring help to the suffering, bring knowledge to the darkened minds. They are always looking out into the world to find one soul that is willing and ready to be helped; always looking over the world in order that They may at once come to the souls that are ready to receive Them, and will not shut the doors of their hearts against Them. For our hearts are closed against Them and fast-locked, so that They cannot enter. They may not break down the doors and come in by force. If a man choose his own way and if he lock the doors, none other may turn the key; we are locked up by worldly desire; we are locked up by grasping after the things of the earth; we are locked up with the keys of sin and indifference and sloth; and the Teacher stands waiting till the door be opened in order that He may cross the threshold and illuminate the mind.

Do you say: How do They know among the myriads of men one soul that works for Them and makes itself fit for Their coming? The answer was once given in the form of a picture; that as a man standing on a mountain-top looking over the adjacent valley sees a light in a single cottage because the light shines out against the surrounding darkness, so does the soul that has made itself ready show the light in the darkness of the surrounding world which catches the eye of the Watcher on the mountain-side and draws His attention by its own light. You must light the soul, in order that the Teacher may see it. He stands watching, but you must give the signal in order that He may become your Teacher and guide you on the way. How great the need you will perhaps understand better at the end of the remaining work that lies before us, as I trace the work of the disciple and what may really be done by him; but let me leave you this morning with this thought in your minds: that the Teacher is watching, is waiting, is desiring to find you, desiring to teach you: that you have the power to draw Him to you, that only you can let Him come. He may knock at the door of your heart, but you must cry out the word that bids Him enter; and if you would follow the path I have traced for you this morning, if step by step you would thus learn control of mind, meditation, building of character, there you would have spoken the threefold word which makes it possible for the Teacher to reveal Himself. When that word is breathed out in the silence of the soul then the Master appears before it, and the feet of the Guru are found.

# THE LIFE OF THE DISCIPLE

## THE PROBATIONARY PATH.   THE FOUR INITIATIONS

IT is a difficult task, my brothers, that lies before us this morning.  In the two preceding lectures I have been dealing with the life of men in the world, and pointing out to you how in this ordinary life men might gradually prepare themselves for the higher stages of evolution; how they might gradually train themselves for swifter progress, for swifter advance.  But today we have to go outside the life of man in the ordinary sense of the term—not so far as the outer appearance is concerned, but so far as the reality of the inner life is to be studied.  For the stages of human progress that we are now to deal with are distinct and definite stages, which lead men out of the life of the world into the life of the higher regions; out of the ordinary humanity into a humanity which is divine.  And inasmuch, therefore, as it must take us more outside common experience, the task is, as I say, more difficult, both for you who hear it and for myself who speak.  For in these higher matters higher faculties must needs be brought into play; and they best will be able to follow this lofty teaching who, at least, have tried to some extent that purification of life and building of character to which our last two mornings have been devoted in thought.

I brought you yesterday up to the point at which a man, having tried to improve his life and control his thought, to bring himself into preparation for discipleship, has drawn the attention of some great Teacher, has drawn the attention of a Guru, so that he may now begin the first stages of discipleship. And it is these first stages that we will take in beginning this morning. However large the subject, I have to try to run through the whole of the life of discipleship, of chelâship, this morning.

The first stages make up what has been called "the probationary path," that is the stage of probationary as separated from the stage of accepted chelâship. In the probationary path, while we can recognize certain stages, and the acquirement of certain definite qualifications, we do not find them so definitely marked out as are those of what we will call the Path proper—that of chelâship recognized and distinct. In the true Path, the Path where the disciple is not only recognized by his Master, but recognizes his Master, in that Path the four stages are exceedingly distinct, are known by separate names, and are separated by distinct Initiations. On the probationary path the stages are marked, but they are not separated in that distinct way. The stages may be said rather to run side by side than successively and one after the other. The probationary chelâ, as we may call one entering on the stages of this path, is not expected to perform perfectly everything he begins to practice. He is expected to attempt, but perfect performance is not demanded from him. It is sufficient if he be in earnest, if his efforts are sustained, if he does not change his mind nor lose sight of his goal. Many allowances, as we say in human affairs, are made for him on the ground of human frailty, human weakness, and the lack of knowledge which hinders his advance. The trials he meets with, the tests he undergoes, are the trials and tests which are met with in ordinary life, troubles of every kind and form, on which I shall have a word to say presently, but they are not of the nature of those which belong to the distinct and definite Path. The stages of the probationary path, if I remember rightly, were traced some years ago from the well-known Hindu teachings, by a Brâhmana, then in England, and a member of the Theosophical Society, Mohini Mohun Chatterji of Calcutta; he recounted what have been called the preliminary steps which men must take and must accomplish, helped to a certain extent by their Teachers, but for the most part unconsciously to themselves—that is, as far as their waking consciousness is concerned; the chelâ appears to himself to be treading the path alone, and to be dependent on his own strength and energy. I need not say that this is an illusion due to his own blindness and ignorance, for the eyes of his Teacher are on him, although it may not be known to him in his waking consciousness, and help is ever extended to him from the higher planes of being, help that shows itself in this life, although it may not show itself clearly to his waking mind. And now we shall find the qualifications we have dealt with as preparatory in a general sense take to themselves more definite shapes on the probationary path.

The first qualification is the outcome of the experiences through which he has passed; they awake and train in him VIVEKA, or discrimination. Discrimination between the real and the unreal, between the eternal and the transitory. Until this appears he will be bound to the earth by ignorance, and worldly objects will exercise over him all their seductive glamor. His eyes must be opened, he must pierce through the veil of Mâyâ, at least sufficiently to rate earthly things at their true value, for from Viveka is born the second of the qualifications—

VAIRAGYA. I have already pointed out to you that a man must begin to train himself in separation from action as regards its fruit. He must train himself to do action as a duty without continually looking for any sort of personal gain. That training we will suppose has been carried out by a man certainly for life after life, before

the demand is made on him which he must answer
to a very considerable extent before Initiation is
possible, that he shall become definitely indifferent
to earthly objects. Indifference to earthly objects,
indifference to worldly objects, Vairâgya, is the
second of the qualifications in the probationary
path of chelâship. He has developed Viveka and,
as we have seen, this means the discrimination between the real and the unreal, between the transitory and the permanent. And as reality and
permanency make themselves felt in the man's
mind, it is inevitable that worldly objects shall lose
their attraction, and that he shall become definitely
indifferent to them. When the real is seen the
unreal is so unsatisfactory; when the permanent
is recognized, if only for a moment, the transitory
seems so little worth striving after; in the probationary path all the objects around us lose their
attractive power, and it is no longer an effort for
the man to turn away from them; it is no longer
by deliberate effort of the will that he does not
permit himself to work for fruit. The objects have
no longer an attraction in themselves; the root of
desire is gradually perishing, and these objects, as
it is said in the *Bhagavad Gîtâ*, turn away from
the abstemious dweller in the body. It is not so
much that he deliberately abstains, as that they
lose the power to any way satisfy him. The objects
of the senses turn away from him, because of that

training that we have already dealt with, that he has passed through.

Seeing objects then in their transitory character it is quite natural that out of indifference to the objects should also grow, as a matter of course, that which he has long been striving after, namely, indifference to their fruits; for the fruits are themselves but other objects. The fruits themselves share the impermanency and unreality which he recognizes, having seen the real and the permanent.

And then the third of the qualifications has to be gained on the probationary path: SHATSAMPATTI, the sixfold group of mental qualities or mental attributes which show themselves within the life of this chelâ-candidate—as perhaps we may call him. He has long been striving to rule his thoughts in the manner with which we are familiar. He has been practicing all those methods which we spoke of yesterday, to gain self-control, to acquire the habit of meditation, and to perform the building of character. These have prepared him now to show forth in the real man—for we are concerned with the real man and not with the illusory appearance—to show forth in the real man, *Shama,* control of the mind, that definite regulation of thought, that definite understanding of the effects of thought, and of his relation to the world around him, as he affects it for good or for evil by his own thinking. By the recognition of that power that he has either to help or to mar by his own thought the lives of other men, how to hinder or to help the evolution of the race, he becomes a deliberate worker for human progress and for the progress of all evolving beings within the limits of the world to which he belongs. And this regulation of thought—now a definite attitude of the mind—is preparing him, as we shall see, for complete and definite chelâship, where every thought is to be made the instrument of the Master's work, and where comparatively without effort the mind is to run along the grooves that are traced for it by the will.

Out of that regulation of thought, now so largely accomplished, follows inevitably *Dama*, control of the senses and the body, that which we may call regulation of conduct. Do you notice how, when dealing with things from the occult standpoint, they are reversed as compared with the standpoint of earth? Worldly men think more of conduct than of thought. The occultist thinks far more of thought than of conduct. If the thought be right the conduct must inevitably be pure; if the thought be regulated, the conduct must inevitably be well controlled and governed. The outer appearance or action is only the translation of the inner thought which in the world of form takes shape as what we call action; but the form is dependent on the life within, the shape is dependent on the moulding energy which makes it. The Arûpa world is the

world of causes, the Rûpa world is only the world
of effects; and therefore if we regulate thought
the conduct must be regulated, as it is the natural
and inevitable expression of thought.

The third mental attribute that marks this attitude of the inner man is *Uparati,* best translated
perhaps as a wide and noble and sustained tolerance—I use that word in the very widest sense
that you can give to it—tolerance of all that is
round him, a kind of sublime patience which is
able to wait, which is able to understand, and,
therefore, demands from none more than he can
give. This again is the preparation for a very distinct stage on the path of full chelâship. This
attitude of the man, the tolerant attitude, is able
to make allowances for every one and everything,
looks on all men not as they are seen from without but as they are seen from within, sees their
aspirations, their desires and their motives, and not
only the clumsy mistranslations which appearance
often gives in the outer world. He learns tolerance
of all different forms of religion, tolerance of all
different kinds of custom, tolerance of all the varying traditions of men. He understands that all
these are transitory phases which men ultimately
outgrow, and he is not so unreasonable as to expect
from the child humanity that wideness, that
breadth, that sense of dignified patience which is
characteristic of humanity in its manhood and not
in its early stages. This attitude of the mind must

be constantly cultivated by the man who is approaching initiation, and he must gain that tolerance by insight into truth and be able to recognize the underlying truth underneath the veil of misleading appearances. Do you notice how all through it is the dawning of the sense of reality that is the great change that has come over the man in this probationary path? He is no longer deceived by appearances as he was in the early days. As he grows he sees reality and so gradually gets rid of illusion. He is shaking off subjection to appearances, and he is recognizing truth, no matter what may be its illusory form.

The next point in his mental attitude is *Titiksha*, endurance, a patient bearing of all that comes, a total absence of resentment. You will remember how I drew your attention to this as a thing to strive for, how a man was gradually to get rid of the tendency to feel injured, how he was to cultivate love and compassion and forgiveness, and the result of that cultivation of the mind is this mental attitude, steady and defined. The inner man thus gets rid of resentment—resentment towards everything, towards men, towards circumstances, towards everything that surrounds him in life. Why? Because he sees truth and he knows the Law, and therefore knows that whatever circumstances surround him, they are the outcome of the good Law. He knows that whatever men may do to him they are only the unconscious agents of the Law. He knows that whatever comes to him in life is of his own creating in the past. And so his attitude is the attitude of absence of resentment. He realizes justice, therefore he cannot be angry with anything, for nothing can touch him which he has not deserved; nothing can come in his way which he has not put there in his former lives. Thus we find that no troubles and no joys can turn him aside from his path; he is no longer to be changed in direction by anything that comes in his way. He sees the path and treads it; he sees the goal and presses towards it. He is no longer following devious and indefinite ways, here, there and everywhere; but firmly, steadily, he follows the path he has chosen. He cannot be attracted away from it by pleasure; he cannot be driven away from it by pain. He cannot be discouraged by dullness, by voidness, by emptiness; he cannot be induced to stray from it by offers from any save the one Guru whose Feet he seeks. Incapacity to be turned aside, strong in endurance—ah! there is a quality he needs indeed on this probationary path. For I spoke of the tests and ordeals which will beset his way, and it is well that you should understand why these difficulties should come. The man who has entered on the probationary path intends to accomplish within a very limited number of lives what the man of the world will accomplish in hundreds upon hundreds of lives. He is like the man who, wanting to reach the top of the mountain, refuses to follow the track that winds round and round. He says: "I am going straight up the mountain-side, I am not going to waste my time on this winding beaten track which will take me so long, the slow way on which most of the going is smooth and easy, beaten by the myriads of feet that tread it. I shall go by the shorter route, I shall take the swifter path, I shall go straight up the mountain-side. No matter what the difficulties, I will climb the mountain. No matter what obstacles there may be, I will go; precipices there may be—I will cross them; walls of rock there may be—I will climb them; obstacles and boulders in my path there may be—I will manage in some way to surmount them or get round them; but up that mountain-side I mean to travel." What will be the result? He will find a thousand-fold more difficulties surround him on the path. If he gains in time he must pay in trouble for the difficulty of the achievement. The man who enters on the probationary path is the man who chooses the short way to the mountain-top, and calls down on himself the whole of his past Karma, which is largely to be got rid of before he is fitted for initiation. The great Lords of Karma who administer the karmic Law—those mighty Intelligences high above us, greater than our comprehension can understand, greater than our reason can in any way fathom, who have been spoken of as the Recorders of Karma, Those who keep the âkâshic records in which are written

down all the past thoughts and deeds of men—
They have, as it were, an account of each individual. They have before Their omniscient eyes the
life-record of each man, and that record which lies
under Their eyes has to be mostly discharged, ere
he passes through the portals of initiation. And
when he enters on the probationary path, when
deliberately of his own set will he puts his feet on
that path, the very putting of his feet there is a
cry to the great Lords of Karma that They will
balance up the account that there is against him,
and present him with the karmic debt he is obliged
to discharge. Is it then any wonder that difficulties grow round his path? The Karma that would
have spread over hundreds of lives will have to be
passed through in a few, perhaps in one, and so
naturally the path is difficult to tread. Family
troubles come round the man, business troubles
press upon him, troubles of mind and of body assail
him; do you wonder then that I said he needs
steadfastness, in order to proceed along the probationary path and not turn back, in order not to be
discouraged? It may seem that everything is
against him. It may seem to him that his Master
has forsaken him. Why, when he is trying his
best, should the worst befall him? Why, when he
is living better than he ever lived before, should all
these difficulties and pains assail him? It seems
so unjust, it seems so hard, it seems so cruel, that
when he is living more nobly than he has ever tried

to live before, he finds himself more hardly treated than ever before by Destiny. He must stand the test, he must refuse to allow any sense of injustice to penetrate into his inner life. He must say to himself: "It was my own doing, I challenged my Karma; what wonder then that I am asked to pay it." And at least he has the encouragement of re-membering that the debt once paid is paid for ever, once lived through no more of it can come to disturb him. Every karmic debt he pays is struck from off life's ledger for evermore. That debt at least is done with. So that if illness strikes him down, he thinks it is well that that much trouble should be gotten rid of; if pain and anxiety assail him, he thinks it is well; he answers: "It will be behind me in the past and not before me in the future." And so it is that in the midst of sorrow he is joyful, in the midst of discouragement he is hopeful, in the midst of pain he is at ease, for the inner man is content with the Law, he is satisfied with the answer which has come to his demand. If there were no answer, it would mean that his voice had not reached the ears of the Great Ones, it would mean his prayer had fallen back to earth; for this trouble is the answer to his petition. Thus in these struggles, these difficulties, these efforts, he gains the fifth mental attribute and that is:—

*Shraddhâ*, faith, or we may call it confidence—confidence in his Master and in himself. You can understand how that will be the result of such a struggle. You can understand how on the further side of the struggle confidence must come out, as the flower must open under the stimulating influence of sunshine and rain. He has learned confidence in his Guru, for has He not led him through all this thorny path and brought him to the other side where the gateway of initiation begins to open in front of him? And he has learned confidence in himself—not in his lower self whose weakness he has conquered, but in his divine Self whose strength he is beginning to recognize. For he understands that every man is divine, he understands that what his Guru is to-day, he himself is going to become in the lives that still stretch out in front of him. And the confidence he feels in the power of the Master to teach and to guide him, in the wisdom of the Master to lead and to instruct him; and a confidence in himself, most humble yet most strong, that inasmuch as he is himself divine, he also has the power to accomplish; that however much of effort may be needed, however much of difficulty still remains to conquer, the strength that is in him is one with Brahman, and is enough for every difficulty, enough for every trial.

The sixth mental attribute is *Samâdhâna*, balance, composure, peace of mind, that equilibrium and steadiness which result from the attainment of the foregoing qualities. With the gaining of this the probationary path is trodden, the chelâ-candidate stands ready before the gateway, and there appears without a further effort the fourth qualification :—

MUMUKSHA, the desire for emancipation, the wish to gain liberation, that which, crowning the long efforts of the candidate, shows him to be an Adhikari, to be ready for initiation. He has been proved and not found wanting: his discrimination is keen, his indifference is no temporary disgust, due to a passing disappointment, his mental and moral character is lofty—he is fit, he is ready for initiation. No more is asked, he stands fit to come face to face with his Master, face to face with the life that he so long has sought.

Notice ere we put our hand on the gateway of initiation that every quality of the probationary path is a preparation for what lies in front, is a moral and mental quality. Moral and mental qualities are the qualifications that are demanded—not powers, as they are called, not abnormal psychic development, not the Siddhis. These are not in any sense demanded or required. A man may have gained some of the Siddhis and yet not be fit for initiation; but he must have the moral qualifications. These are demanded with a rigidity that nothing can change—with a rigidity, let me say in passing, that is the result of experience. For the great Gurus in Their vast experience of humanity, have been training it step by step for myriads of years. They know well enough that the qualification for true discipleship must be found in the

mind and in the moral character and not in the
development of the psychic nature; that has to
come in its own place and in its own good time.
But to be a recognized disciple, an accepted chelâ,
the mind and morals must be fitted to meet the
gaze of the Guru; such as have been stated are the
qualifications He demands, and these His pupils
must give Him ere the second birth will be granted
by Him who alone can give it. And notice also that
these imply knowledge and devotion—the growth
of knowledge that the man may see, and the growth
of devotion without which the path cannot be trodden. And, therefore, it is written in the Upanishad
that knowledge unallied to devotion is not enough,
that devotion by itself is not sufficient; it must be
knowledge wedded to devotion, for these are the
two wings by which the disciple rises.

We come to the Path itself. Of the great Initiations which mark the stages of the Path after the
chelâ is accepted by his Guru and when the Guru
takes upon Himself the guidance and instruction
and guardianship of His chelâ—of these great
Initiations from time to time a word has been
dropped from the lips of some Teacher in the outer
world, and we can find hints thrown out here and
there, hints which are verified by the experience of
those who pass within the gateway, hints which are
permitted to be expanded to some small extent, not
for the gratification of idle curiosity, but for the
training of those who would fain prepare them-

selves for this great step in advance. What can be said about them must obviously be imperfect; that which can be revealed in the world of men of these great mysteries can only be fragmentary information. Many questions will rise in your mind as I take these hints and weave them together into a slight but connected whole. Many questions will rise in your minds the answers to which could not be wisely given. The whole object, as I say, of giving the information is not to gratify curiosity, it is not in order that a man may ask a number of questions and get answers given to them one after another; the hints that are given are meant for men who are in earnest, for those who want to know in order that they may prepare, for those who want to understand in order that they may be able to accomplish. And so from time to time these hints are given, the partial information which is enough for immediate guidance, but not enough to satisfy mere idle and worldly curiosity.

Two mighty Teachers stand out in history as having given more information on this subject than any others—each of Them a Teacher of a world-wide religion—world-wide not in the sense of area, but world-wide in their bearing on the souls that are ready for their reception. One of these great Teachers was the Founder of Buddhism, the LORD BUDDHA; and the other of these Teachers was SHRI SHANKARACHARYA, who did for Hinduism what we may say the BUDDHA did for countries beyond its

reach in founding His exoteric faith. As regards
the Path Their teachings are identical, as the teachings of every such great Initiate must needs be.
Each of Them laid down the same stages; each of
Them marks the stages by definite initiations which
separate each stage from those which precede it
and those which follow it. In the teaching itself
there is perfect identity, it is only in the phrase-
ology adapting it respectively to one faith or the
other that differences arise. Here again, of course,
is one of the reasons why men must learn to seek
truth under diverse forms and appearances, otherwise they quarrel about the forms instead of realizing the identity that underlies these outer labels
that are merely names.

Four different stages there are, as I say, and
each of them marked by an initiation. Now initiation means this; it means the expansion of consciousness which is brought about by the definite
intermediation of the Guru, who acts in place of
the one GREAT INITIATOR of humanity and gives the
second birth in His Name. This expansion of consciousness is the note as it were of initiation, for
this expansion of consciousness gives what is called
"the key of knowledge"; it opens up to the Initiate
new vistas of knowledge and of power, it places
within his hand the key which unlocks the doors of
nature. To what end? In order that he may become more serviceable to the world at large; in
order that his power for service may be increased;

in order that he may join that scanty band of men who are vowed to humanity and who have re-nounced the lower self, who seek nothing save the service of the Master and of humanity; who know that the service of the Master and of humanity is one and the same service; who have done with the world and everything that the world can offer; who have dedicated themselves for ever to the service of the Great Ones to be Their instruments of work, the channels of Their help and of Their grace. And between each of the great Initiations certain definite things have to be done—changes in the inner man—but with a great difference from the changes which have hitherto been considered. When a man is once initiated, what is done has to be done perfectly, no longer imperfectly; every ac-complishment is completely achieved, every chain is definitely cast off. No longer the imperfect working out; he cannot pass onwards till perfectly the work of the stage is accomplished. So that there is this definiteness about it, which is nowhere else in life, that each successive stage is finished before the man passes further. No half-work, no incomplete achievement is here accepted. How-ever long it may take, the work must be absolutely finished before another step forward can be taken. Technically that has been called "the casting off of the fetter," of certain things that still bind the soul. At the end of the Path lies Jîvanmukti; to have trodden it is to reach that stage where life is free, so that every fetter must be cast off wholly in order that nothing may bind the living man.

The first great Initiation makes the man what is called by SHRI SHANKARACHARYA the parivrajaka—what is called by the BUDDHA the Srotâpatti. The Buddhist word, generally given in its Pâlî form, means "he who has entered the stream" which separates him from this world. He no longer belongs to this world, though he may live in it; he has here no place, nothing can hold him. Exactly the same idea is conveyed by the word Parivrajaka, a man who wanders about, that is, who has no settled home; not necessarily wandering about in the body, not necessarily no settled home in the body—as it has come to mean in the exoteric sense—but the man who in his inner life is separated from the world, who has in this transitory world no fixed place of abode, to whom in this transitory world one place is not different from any other. He can go here, there and everywhere, where his Master may send him. No place has power to hold him, no place has power to bind him; he has shaken off the fetters of place. And so he is called "the wanderer." I know of course, as you know, that this stage is taken in quite an exoteric sense to-day; but I am taking it in the inner sense, in the meaning of the Great Ones who gave it. We know, alas! how much things have changed from the older days; how that which was then a reality in life has now become a matter of

words and of outer appearance. But I am anxious
that you should know the four stages of the Path
as they are spoken of in Hinduism, as some people
imagine that they were revealed only by the LORD
BUDDHA, whereas He but proclaimed again the
ancient narrow Path, that all Initiates of the One
Lodge have trodden, are treading, and shall tread.

Let me take the reality first. The man who has
crossed the stream, as I said, has definitely parted
with the world—he wants no more of it except as
he can serve it. He asks no more of it except as
in it he can do his Guru's bidding. That is the
mark of the first great Initiation—of the man who
is re-born. For the most part the re-birth takes
place outside the body but in waking consciousness:
*i.e.*, the man is initiated generally in his astral body
in full consciousness, the physical body being left
entranced; occasionally a chelâ is initiated without
the waking consciousness being permitted for a
time to share in the knowledge. But in either case
the act can never be undone; the man can never
again be as he was before. The babe, when it is
born into the world, may for a time be unconscious
of the new world around it, but that babe cannot
return into its mother's womb and be as though no
birth had been passed through. So neither can
the Initiate who has passed through the second
birth ever again be as though he had not been thus
born, and share in the life of the outer world as
those who have not passed the second birth may

share in it. He may delay in his progress, he may be slow in his advance, he may take a longer time than is necessary to throw off the fetters that still bind him; but he can never again be uninitiated, the key can never again pass out of his grasp. He has stepped into the stream; he is separated from the world; he must go forward however slowly, however many lives he may spend in the doing.

A question has been raised as to the number of lives intervening between this step and final liberation, the attainment of Jîvanmukti. I remember hearing that Svâmi T. Subba Row, speaking here to some friends about the general idea that seven lives had to be passed in this division of chelâship, made the perfectly true and significant remark: "It may be seven lives or seventy, it may be seven days or seven hours." That is: the life of the soul is not counted by mortal years or by mortal time; it depends on its energy, on its strength, on its will to succeed. A man may waste his time or spend it to the best advantage, and according to that will be the progress that he will make.

But during this stage, which is commenced by the first great Initiation and is closed by the second, there are three different things that a man must get absolutely rid of ere he can pass the second portal. The first of these is the illusion of the personal self. Personality must be destroyed; no longer now controlled, no longer now diminished, no longer kept in check: but destroyed, killed for evermore. The illusion of the separated personal self has to go. The chelâ must recognize himself as one with all other selves, for the Self of all is one. He must realize that all around him, man, the animal and plant worlds, the mineral and elemental forms of life, are all one. The illusion of personality must be gotten rid of. See how the extending consciousness will help in this; how the recognition of the true Self will make it possible to get rid of the false; how the seeing of the Real will cause the disappearance of the unreal; and so the illusion of the personal self is absolutely killed. Why? because his eyes are opened and they pierce through the illusion; thus he becomes free and casts off the fetter called "the delusion of self."

And he must get rid of doubt. That is the second obstacle that will prevent him from going further. But he has to get rid of doubt in a very definite way—he is to get rid of doubt by knowledge. No longer to him are the things of the invisible world to be questions of speculation; no longer to him are the great truths of religion to be philosophic ideas. They are to be realized facts. He must no longer have any question in his mind as to how is this or why? There are certain fundamental truths of life on which no longer possibility of doubt must remain to him. Ere he can go one step further forward, he must be absolutely convinced beyond the possibility of question of the great truth of Re-incarnation; he must know beyond the possibility of question the great truth of Karma; he must know beyond the possibility of question the great truth of existence of the divine Men, of the Jîvanmuktas, who are the Gurus of humanity. On these points no possibility of doubt must remain; that is, he must have knowledge no longer theoretical but real, no longer theoretical but practical, so that no shade of questioning on these can ever again possibly cloud his mind; the only position that is thus secure is where knowledge replaces speculation, and where absolute contact with the reality makes impossible any more the deceptions that are caused by the illusions of the outer world.

The last of these three fetters that he has to entirely cast off at this stage is superstition. Realize clearly what that means and then you will understand very fully why both SHRI SHANKARACHARYA and the BUDDHA used the names that They respectively gave for this stage of chelâship. Superstition means this, in the technical sense (in which I am, of course, now using the word): it means the reliance on external sectarian rites and ceremonies for spiritual help. So far as their external nature is concerned, the man recognizes the truth beneath the form, and if the truth be there the value of the outer shape depends on its adaptation to this world of ignorance and illusion. The man has risen above exoteric forms and ceremonies. But you are familiar with this idea in your everyday life. The

Sannyâsî is supposed to be a man who is risen above these things, and from whom they are no longer demanded. And why not? Because he is supposed to have touched reality, because he is supposed no longer to have any need of these things which are the rungs of the ladder by which men must climb; they are necessary in the earlier stages—do not forget that fact—this is a case of growth. If you would mount to the top of the house you must mount by the staircase or ladder, and foolish would be the man who said, "I will not climb by the staircase or steps," unless that man had such power and such knowledge of the laws of nature that he was able to change the polarity of his body and rise by what is called levitation—by the action of the will instead of by the comparatively slow and clumsy method of going up step by step. For such a man the staircase is unnecessary because he can rise upward by his own power, and reach the top of the house without the slow method of climbing. But it does not therefore follow that the staircase is useless; it does not therefore follow that other men can reach the top of the house by refusing to use the staircase. And too many men to-day, who are unable to raise themselves, refuse to use the staircase, forgetting that until the will is developed the lower forms are necessary if the man is to rise at all.

And this brings me to say a word on the "true Sannyâsî." Even five thousand years ago the word was used without the reality. Even five thousand years ago, at the beginning of the Kali Yuga, we find Shrî Krishna drawing a distinction between the Sannyâsî in appearance and the Sannyâsî in reality. Do you remember how speaking on this very subject he said: "He that performeth action as duty, independently of the fruit of action, he is a Sannyâsî, and he is a Yogî; not he that is without fire and who doeth nothing?" You know the meaning of the technical phrase, "he that is without fire," that is, he who does not light the sacrificial fires, who does not perform rites and ceremonies; for from the Sannyâsî these are not demanded. But, said Shrî Krishna, he is not the true Sannyâsî who is known only by the absence of rites and ceremonies and by the absence of his actions in the world of men. And if this were true five thousand years ago, it is far more true, alas! to-day. If it were true when the great Avatâra was treading the plains of India, it is far more true when five thousand years of darkness have elapsed. When we glance over the whole of the Eastern world, if we take India herself with her countless Sannyâsîs, we see men who are Sannyâsîs by the cloth and not by the life, men who are Sannyâsîs by outer appearance and not by inner renunciation. And if we leave Indian soil and tread that say of Ceylon, Burma, China or Japan, there too we find Buddhist monks who are monks by the yellow robe and not by the noble life, in the external appear-

ance and not in the internal truth. And although
it is still true that religion is easier to live here
than in any other land; although it is still true
that the traditions of India make her very soil
sacred and her very atmosphere more spiritual
than the atmosphere of other lands; although there
are places so holy through the lives that have been
led in them that even for the worldly man to go to
them quiets the mind and wakes up the aspirations
of the soul; although all this is true of India, and
therefore she is beloved and sacred evermore, alas!
her children are unworthy of her possibilities, and
they have fallen on every side. Looking over the
world of men we see no place where the spiritual
life is generally led, no nation where this is recognized as supreme. The heart might go well-nigh
to breaking that knows the possibilities and sees
the actualities, that knows what might be and sees
what is, that knows the truth and sees, alas! the
lie that simulates the truth. And yet, despite all,
no disciple's heart need break, for the Masters live
for evermore and Their disciples also still tread the
world of men; but now their discipleship is shown
not in the outer garb, but in the inner life, not in
the mere cloth that is worn, but in the knowledge,
the purity and the devotion which still open the
gateway of Initiation.

So we come onward to the second stage called
by SHRI SHANKARACHARYA the Kutichaka, the man
who builds a hut, called by the Buddhists the

Sakridâgâmin, the man who receives birth once more. This stage is one in which no definite fetters are cast off, but certain acquirements are made. Here comes in the place of the Siddhis. After the second Initiation it is necessary that the Siddhis should be developed, because the disciple has reached a stage of his life in which he must be capable of very extended service, in which he must be able to do his Master's work not only in the world of physical men, but also in the other worlds that surround it and lie outside the physical plane. He must be able not only to speak with the lips but also to speak directly from mind to mind with conscious and deliberate intention. I shall try to show you to-morrow what are the possibilities of service that lie before him, which re-act on the physical world, and which, if they were thoroughly accomplished, as they are not to-day, would largely change the trend even of the physical life of man. But in order that he may do this part of the work, in order that he may prepare himself for the lofty tasks that lie before him when all knowledge will be open to him, and Nature will have no veil able to blind his eyes, he must at this stage develop his inner faculties and unfold one by one those inner possibilities of the man. It is at this stage that it is necessary, if it has not been done before, that the inner fire should be awakened, it is here that Kundalinî must be roused to function in the physical body and in the astral body of the living man.

You can read about it in some books, as in the *Ânanda Lahiri* of SHRI SHANKARACHARYA, of the awakening of the living fire, of the leading it from chakram to chakram; as it wakes up it gives the man the power to leave the physical body at will for as it is led from chakram to chakram it disengages the astral from the physical and sets it free. Then without break of consciousness, without any chasm of blankness separating one world from the other, a man is able to pass out of the physical body into the invisible world, and is able to work there in full consciousness and to bring back all knowledge of the work that he has there accomplished. It is within the second stage that all these powers are developed and evolved, if they have not been evolved earlier, and until they are in full working order, until they are entirely at the command of the chelâ, until there are no barriers left between the visible and invisible world, he cannot pass on. As those barriers break away by the unfolding of the inner senses and powers of the man, by the gaining of the Siddhis, he becomes ready for the third great step in his progress, ready to pass onwards into the next higher stage of being. You will readily understand how easily mischief may be done to unfit men who try to artificially bring about this stage before they are spiritually developed, before the time when they should reach it in orderly evolution. In published writings there are many hints thrown out, especially in the Tântrika books, which are greedily seized on by those who desire to possess powers, and care little for their moral and mental ability to wield those powers aright. In many of the Tantras there are underlying truths for those who can reach them, but the statements on the surface are often exceedingly misleading from their incompleteness for those who do not know the real facts, and who have no Guru to explain blinds and to fill up gaps. And so people—ignorantly taking these up to practice, with the object of forcing their psychical development before their mental and moral development has fitted them to do it with safety—very often bring about results indeed, but results which work for evil and not for good. They often ruin their physical health, they often lose their mental balance, they often injure their intellectual faculties, because they are trying to pluck the fruit of the tree of life before it is ripe for the plucking; because with hands unclean and senses unpurified they try to penetrate into the Holy of Holies. Within that fane the atmosphere is such that nothing unclean can live in it; its vibrations are so powerful, that it breaks in pieces everything which is set in a lower key; it shivers all that is impure, all that is not able to adapt itself to that subtle and tremendous motion.

When, however, under the training of his Guru —for only thus should it even be attempted— when under the training of his Guru the disciple

has completely accomplished this stage, then comes
the third great Initiation, that which makes the
man what SHRI SHANKARACHARYA called a Hamsa,
what is called in the Buddhist literature an
Anâgâmin, the man who receives birth no more,
save indeed by his own free will. This stage is one
—as the name given by SHRI SHANKARACHARYA implies—in which the man realizes unity, in which he
knows that he is one with the SUPREME. The name
is given because in his expanding consciousness he
had already risen into the region in the universe
where that identity is realized, and had experienced "I am it." With the perfecting of his
psychic senses and their correlation with the physical, he is able not only to penetrate the region
where consciousness is felt as a unity, but he is also
able to bring back the memory of that consciousness into his waking hours, to impress it on his
physical brain. Need it be said that the last shred
of earthly desire must needs now fall away from
him if at this stage any shred still remains. So
that in this stage a fetter is cast off which is called
Kâmarâga, desire, little of earth indeed as there
can be in it; but with that realizing of the unity
of all, everything that is separate in appearance
loses its power to deceive for evermore. He has
risen far far above the limitations of separateness,
and so he stands above not only what here we
should call earthly desires, but above the most
highly refined, the most spiritual desires which

have in them aught for the separated self; even spiritual desires fall away from the man who reaches such a height; he cannot separate himself in thought from others, therefore he cannot have spiritual desires for himself as separate, for himself save as part of the whole. Everything that he gains, he gains for all; everything that he wins, he wins for all. He stands in a region of the Universe whence strength comes down into the world of men, and as he gains it he passes it on, he sheds it on all, he shares it with all. Thus all the world is better for each man who reaches this stage. All he wins is won for humanity, and all that comes into his hands comes only to pass through them into the wider world of men. He is one with BRAHMAN, and therefore one with every manifestation; and he is that in his own consciousness, and not only in hope and aspiration. A strange word is here used to describe the other chain that he casts off in this stage—the Pâlî word Patigha, which in English we are obliged to translate as "hatred," although the English word is absurd in this connection. What it really means is this: that inasmuch as he has become one with all he no longer feels the distinctions between races and families, between all the differentiated objects in the world. He no longer can either love or hate because of external distinctions. He can no longer love or hate because a person belongs to a different race. He can no longer love or hate because he draws dis-

tinctions between men and the things around them.
You remember that strange phrase of SHRI
KRISHNA, when he speaks of the Sage making no
distinction between the illuminated Brâhmana and
a dog. He has reached unity, he sees BRAHMAN in
everything. Or to take another phrase: he sees
SHRI KRISHNA everywhere, and the outer garment
of the Lord makes no difference to his purified
vision; therefore he is absolutely without what we
are obliged to call "hatred" or "repulsion."
Nothing repels him, nothing drives him back. He
is love and compassion to everything, love and
compassion to all. He spreads round him as it
were an all-embracing circle of affection. All that
come near him, all that approach him, feel the influence of his divine compassion. And that is why
in the days when Brâhmanas were really all that
their name implies, it was said of the Brâhmana
that he was "the friend of everything, of every
creature." The heart being one with the Divine
was wide enough to enclose within its limits everything that the Divine had made.

Having then cast separateness aside for ever, he
passes into the final stage of chelâship, Parama-
hamsa SHRI SHANKARACHARYA calls it, Arhat is the
Buddist term. Here again one feels the terrible
modern degradation of sacred names, the lofty condition having its name used so widely and so care-
lessly, used so often for mere compliment, for an
outer appearance instead of for a living reality.

The real meaning of this name is that the man has passed the fourth great Initiation, and stands within the stage that precedes Jîvanmukti; in his waking consciousness he can rise to, live in, the Turîya region. He has no need to leave the body to enjoy it. He has no need to leave the body to be conscious in it. His consciousness embraces, has expanded to, that, although at the same time it may be working in the lower brain. And that is one of the great marks of the attainment of that stage. There is no such thing as physical unconsciousness necessary in order that that high region of consciousness may be trodden; for his consciousness has expanded to it, and while he is speaking and talking and living in the world of men, he has all that vast knowledge within his reach and is consciously experiencing it at will. In this stage, he throws off the last five "fetters," that he may become the Jîvanmukta. The first of these is called Rûparâga, desire for "life in form"—no desire for such life can move him. Then, he casts off Arûparâga, desire for "life without form"—no such desire has any power to bind him. And then Mâna is cast away, and again we have to use an English word far too gross to express the real, subtle nature of the fetter cast off—pride; not thinking even for a passing moment of the greatness of his own achievement, of the dizzy altitude at which he stands, for he recognizes neither high nor low, neither lofty height nor lowly vale. He sees and feels them all as one. He casts off next the possibility of being ruffled by anything that may occur. Whatever happens, he will remain unshaken. The spheres may clash together, he will remain unmoved. Nothing that can happen to the manifested world can shake the sublime serenity of the man who has risen thus to the realization of the Self of all. What matters a catastrophe—it is but the form that is broken. What matters the crash of a world—it is but the manifestation that is changing. The eternal, the undying, the ancient and the constant, he lives in That, and there is nothing that can shake his serenity, there is nothing that can mar the perfection of his peace. And then there falls from his limbs the last fetter of all—Avidyâ —that which makes illusion; the last faint film which prevents the perfect insight and the perfect liberty. While he need be born no more, he may take birth if he will; no compulsion can bring him back to earth, but of his own will he can re-incarnate. He brings within his knowledge everything of our planetary ring. He learns all that this manifestation has to teach; not one lesson is left unlearnt, not one secret remains hidden, not one corner exists into which his eye cannot pierce, not one possibility that he is not able to grasp. At the end of this stage all the lessons have been learnt. All the powers have been achieved. He is omniscient, omnipotent, within this planetary chain. He has accomplished the evolution of humanity; he has trodden the last step that humanity shall have taken when the great Manvantara is accomplished and the work of this universe is achieved. There is nothing that is veiled from him, nothing that is not within himself: his consciousness has expanded to take all into himself. He can enter Nirvâna itself at will; and there there is unity, there there is all-consciousness, there, there is the fulness of life. He has reached the goal of humanity; only the last gateway is before him, and that swings open at the sound of his footstep. That gateway passed, he becomes the Jîvanmukta, according to the Hindu phrase, the Asekha Adept, or He who has no more to learn, according to the Buddhist nomenclature. All is known, all is accomplished. Before Him lie open different paths, any one of which he may choose; before Him spread vast possibilities, any one of which He may stretch forth His hand and take. Out of the limits of this planetary chain, outside the limits of our Kosmos, into regions far beyond even our dimmest apprehending, paths lie open that the Jîvanmukta may choose to tread. One path, the most difficult, the hardest of all, though the swiftest, is that which is called the Path of the Great Renunciation. If He chooses that, deliberately looking over the world of men, the Jîvanmukta refuses to leave it, refuses to go away from it, says that He will remain and take to Himself a body again and again, for the teaching and for the helping of man. Once more SHRI

SHANKARACHARYA speaks of those who wait and function until the work is accomplished. Their own task is over indeed, but They have identified Themselves with humanity, and until the evolution of humanity is over They will not pass away from the struggling ranks of men. They are free, but remain in a voluntary bondage; They are liberated, but in a liberation that will not complete itself until others are liberated too. They are the great Masters of Compassion, who live within the reach of men, that humanity may not be an orphan without a father, that the pupils may not be seeking a Guru and find no Guru to instruct. They are Those to whom some of us feel such an intensity of gratitude, because They stay within the sphere of earth though They live in Nirvânic consciousness beyond it, in order that a link may be kept between the higher worlds and the men who are yet unliberated, those to whom the body is still a prison, in whom the life is not yet set free. All are glorious who have reached that lofty level, all are divine who stand where They are standing. But perhaps one may dare to say without irreverence, that the dearest to the heart of humanity, the most closely bound to it by the ties of passionate gratitude for the renunciation made, are Those who might have gone from us but who stay with us, who might have left us orphans but who remain as the Fathers of men. Such are the great Gurus at whose feet we bow; such the great Masters who stand behind the Theosophical Society. They sent Their messenger, H. P. Blavatsky, to bring the message to the world which the world had well-nigh forgotten, to point again to the narrow and ancient Path along which some feet are treading now, along which your feet may tread.

# THE FUTURE PROGRESS OF HUMANITY

## METHODS OF FUTURE SCIENCE. MAN'S COMING DEVELOPMENT

BROTHERS,—The task that lies before us this morning is by no means an easy one.  Hitherto I have been tracing for you the progress of the individual; hitherto I have been trying to show you how a man who thus determined on his future might be able step by step to rise from the life of the world to the life of the disciple, and how he might anticipate the progress of humanity, how he might accomplish in a few short years what the race will accomplish in the course of untold millennia.  But this morning a different task lies before us.  I am going to try to trace for you that progress through the ages.  I am going to try to lay before you, necessarily exceedingly briefly, the great stages of human progress, taking humanity as a whole.  So that we shall, as it were, have a bird's-eye view of evolution, realize not only the past out of which we have grown into the present, but the future that lies before us as a race.  It is the progress of nations with which I propose to deal, the unfolding of humanity with which we are now concerned. And in trying such a flight as that I feel almost as though I were asking you to mount with me upon the back of Vishnu's vehicle, Garuda the mighty bird, and sweep through the atmosphere of untold ages, glancing downwards at the landscapes over which we pass. I feel that I shall leave you and myself well-nigh breathless after the transit. It is easier for me in one way than it is for you, because by often dwelling on the thought it has become more familiar, while to many of you the ground may perhaps be almost strange, and the Theosophical conception of evolution through the ages may be new in its detail. I shall necessarily be compelled to pass rapidly from point to point without elucidation, and shall therefore be sweeping you over many difficulties rather perhaps by the speed of the transit than by a complete and detailed comprehension of the whole. But let me say this to you: I may be mistaken in some of the details that I may give; I may be in error in some of the smaller points of this vast picture; but the outline as a whole is true; it is not mine, it comes from elsewhere; and although the weakness of the representer may cause error in detail, the fundamental accuracy of the sketch is an accuracy on which you may rely.

Man in the vision of the Great Ones who were his earliest Teachers, Rulers, Guides, is not man as he is to-day, for he is not all that he is meant to be, all that he shall yet become. I do not mean by that

that his progress has on the whole been unsatisfactory. It has not. The place in evolution he has reached, surrounded with difficulties, with doubts, with much of suffering, is a place which on the whole, looked at from the highest standpoint, is fairly satisfactory, considering the shortness of the time that lies behind him, short in the divine measurement, although so long measured by mortal years. Certainly man as he is to-day is by no means what man is in the minds that projected his pilgrimage, in the sight of Those who started him on his evolution. He has come downwards; he has passed his lowest point; a mighty climbing lies in front of him, at the end of which humanity, perfected and glorious, shall indeed be very different from what it is to-day, shall be as it was projected in the divine thought.

The universe, you must bear in mind all through, consists of seven great and distinct regions, thrown out as it were from the divine Mind, thrown from within outwards or from above downwards, whichever expression you prefer—a mighty universe in seven planes or regions. Each plane is distinct in its material, although the essence of all is one and the same, Paramâtmâ whence all proceeds. As this outpouring of the divine thought took shape by the divine will in the manifested universe, and as plane after plane was formed, each plane was characterized by the difference of the density of its material, by the difference of the number of enwrappings in which the primal energy was veiled. So that speaking broadly, you may conceive of this great Kosmos with the LOGOS who gave it birth, you may conceive of it as a mighty solar system, the sun representing the LOGOS and, coming outwards, orb after orb, each orb representing a plane of the universe. Those within would be those in which the matter was subtlest and the energy was least fettered; those outside would be those in which the matter was growing denser, and the energy was more crippled by this density of the material by which it was enfolded.

Next you have to realize that each of these regions has its own inhabitants, and that the course of evolution is the sweeping outwards from the center to the circumference and then the returning inwards from the circumference towards the center. As the Great Breath goes outwards and matter comes into existence, becoming denser and denser, there will be a point at which matter will be at its densest and energy at its feeblest, at which form will be at its most rigid and life at its most hidden; so that this outward process will be a process in which matter will be densifying and form will be increasing in rigidity, while life will be becoming more and more veiled in its manifestation. On the other hand when there is the returning of the Breath, the bringing again of this creative activity as it were to the centre, matter will grow more and more subtle, life will become more and more unveiled, until finally the Great Breath will draw in from this manifested Kosmos all the world's experiences that havo been gained. The humanity which was the object and outcome of this evolutionary process will have become divine and ready for yet mightier stages of advance. And following that great sweep outwards, we realize that as we follow it there is as regards the inhabitants a process towards individualization as they pass into denser matter. So that looking at the inhabitants of these planes, as they lie behind us, we shall see what is called the elemental essence gradually taking to itself more and more definite forms; its evolution, being on the descending arc, lies in its becoming more separated and taking more material forms; it is a process downwards into matter, whereas the evolution now of mankind, being on the ascending arc, lies in its rising into unity and taking more subtle forms, for it is a process upwards into the unveiled life.

You may roughly grasp in this way an idea of the Kosmos as a whole, and you will understand that in the planes that are less dense than the physical, we have not only evolving and ascending humanity but also the involving and descending elemental essence. In the mineral world is the turning point, for there the densest stage has been reached. In the upward evolution the mineral and the vegetable kingdoms of this physical world occupy the physical plane and do not pass to a consciousness beyond it; as evolution proceeds the animal world takes one step upwards, and the animal has to live on what is called the astral plane as well as on the physical; man is intended in the thought of his Builders to conquer and occupy during this evolution five out of the seven planes of the universe. He is intended to function and to be master on the physical, to function and to be master on the astral, to function and to be master on the plane above the astral, the mental, which includes the Svarga of the Hindu, the Devachan of the Theosophist; we may use another term that better expresses the whole range of that state of consciousness, the term Sushuptî, a state now known during earth-life only by the exceptionally experienced and developed, but which in the course of evolution will be experienced by the majority of the human race. Above this comes the fourth, or Turîya plane, the plane of Buddhî, and above that yet again the plane of Nirvâna, or Turîya-tîta. So that you get five distinct regions of the Universe which humanity is meant to occupy in the course of this evolution—the physical, the astral, the sushuptic, the turîyic and the nirvânic. Those are the stages of expanding consciousness through which man has to pass, if he is to succeed in the pilgrimage which he has to make. The individual may take these steps more rapidly by Yoga, but the majority of the race is to accomplish this evolution only in the course of ages; not quite the

whole race, but the majority of human kind, ere
this Manvantara is over, will have conquered all
these planes of expanded consciousness and will be
functioning upon the whole five, Man will then
have formed to himself vehicles in which consciousness can work on each plane. And when we look
at man to-day we know that in him there is the
possibility of the unfolding of this fivefold life,
the fivefold vehicles which will occupy these different regions and make him, as he is meant to be,
master and lord of this manifested universe.

Two planes yet lie above and beyond, which will
not be touched by the majority of mankind in this
evolution at all—two planes which are mere names
for us, names conveying no definite meaning, so
high are those spheres beyond our loftiest imagin-
ings. These are that which is spoken of as Paranir-
vâna and that which is still higher, Mahâparanir-
vâna. What these states are we cannot even dream.
These are the seven stages of the Kosmos. Humanity as a majority is to conquer and occupy five of
them, and some of humanity's children will reach
to the yet higher that remain; but for the bulk of
our race its evolution is within the fivefold universe.

That may perhaps give you a hint—I have no
time to work it out in this lecture—as to what
underlay the controversy that arose as to the
"five" and "seven" in Nature. There has been
much dispute as to that, especially between some of

the Theosophists and some of our Brâhmana brothers. The Brâhmanas claimed the fivefold classification, whereas the Theosophists insisted on the sevenfold. The truth is that the total classification is sevenfold as you will find in the sacred Books, the sevenfold fire dividing itself, hinted at here and there in the Upanishads. But the present evolution is an evolution of the fivefold nature only, the evolution symbolized in the five prânas familiar in Hindu literature. I only say this in passing because so many disputes are disputes which need not arise if people understood each other a little better than they do; if instead of fighting over mere appearances they would look beneath the surface, they would generally find a point of union. As I say, I have not time to dwell upon it, but it is here that really lies the key to the riddle of the five and the seven. Mankind as a whole develops five vehicles for the fivefold evolution, whereas those who are the very flower of humanity reach two stages that lie still beyond.

Now studying the evolution of humanity, we find the First and the Second Races employed in the evolution of form, and in the evolution of the lower or animal nature; that is, they developed the physical body with the etheric double (which in theosophical books has been called the Linga Sharîra) and the kâmic or passional nature—that which you find in the animal and also find in man. Coming to the Third Race of humanity we find that special help was given to it when it had reached its mid-most point; it was not that humanity could not have developed in the course of ages without that special help, but that such help enormously quickened the process and made its evolution far more rapid than otherwise it would have been. The great Kumâras, Those who are spoken of as Mânasaputras, Sons of Mind, the first fruits of a past evolution, Those came in humanity in order that They might hasten its growth, might quicken its development, and by throwing out a spark from Their own essence They gave that impulse we have read of, by which Manas, or the individual soul, was born in man.

The outcome of that special help was, as I have said, a great increase in the rapidity of human evolution. And then was formed that vehicle known as Kârana Sharîra, or causal body. It is the "body of Manas" that lasts through the whole life of the re-incarnating soul. It lasts from life to life, carrying on the result of each to the next. Therefore is it called the causal body, because in this body there are the causes which unfold themselves into effects on the lower planes of earthly life.

Now the plan of human development from that time forward is this: the causal body being formed there was a vehicle in which everything could be laid up and accumulated, the receptacle and the storehouse of experience. Passing into earthly life and throwing out, in the way I explained to you before, a projection of itself, its earthly life is spent in the gathering of experience, in the collecting in the physical world of certain facts, certain knowledge, that which as a whole we call the experience of life. Passing through the gateway of death man has to assimilate the experience that he has gathered, and he lives a life out of the body, when he is no longer to be seen in the physical world, but is dwelling on the astral and the devachanic planes that lie beyond it. There he works out certain effects and assimilates the experiences he gathered on earth, working them into his own nature. Each life gives him certain results; these results are taken and worked up into faculties and powers. If a man for instance exercised during his physical life much power of thought, used much effort to understand, to accumulate knowledge, to develop his mind, then during the period that intervenes between death and birth, he is employed in turning all these efforts of his into intellectual capacities, with which he will return from his next birth in this world; so also all his higher aspirations, his spiritual hopes, his spiritual longings, will be worked into the essence of his nature, during the time which intervenes between his death and his next birth. When he returns again to earth he will be born under circumstances which will facilitate his growth, and he will bring with him the developed spiritual capacities which he can use for further development during his next life upon earth.

You see how perfectly regular are the stages of growth in the body that lasts from life to life. The Kârana Sharîra put out a projection from itself on the lower planes, and gathers a harvest of experience; then it withdraws it with its experiences towards itself, letting it remain in the lower regions of Devachan for the assimilation of that experience and the building it into faculty, into power, into capacity; then it withdraws it wholly into itself as the containing vehicle of consciousness; and then comes another putting forth of this now more highly developed life, which shows on the lower planes the powers it has gained in this way. Thus there should be a steady and continuous advance, life after life, the Kârana Sharîra being the receptacle of all the experiences, and being the permanent man into which the whole of these experiences are built.

Realizing that, you will understand what is meant by the "pilgrimage of the soul": each life should find a man greater in his mind, greater in his moral powers, greater in his spiritual faculties. That is the plan of evolution. It is carried out very imperfectly, and hence the enormous length of the pilgrimage. It is carried out with many turns and twists and wanderings into byways and travelling along devious paths, instead of pursuing a straight and upward road. Therefore humanity is long in its journeying and the evolution needs such myriads of millennia to accomplish. None the less it shall be accomplished, for such is the Divine Will for humanity, and that cannot be finally frustrated however much delay may be made in its accomplishment.

Evolution proceeded through the second half of the Third Race and onwards into the Fourth. Now in the Fourth Race grew up that mighty civilization of Atlantis which reached its highest point in the great sub-race of which you have heard a few words even from Western science—the Toltec. It was a civilization which was marvellous in its accomplishments; but there was this difficulty in connection with it. Man was very low down on the ascending arc, and was deeply immersed in matter. His mental faculties were very largely what we should now call psychic, and it was necessary that they should be veiled for a time in order that intellectual power might be evolved and make a higher evolution in the future possible for humanity. Therefore the great kosmic law, that law that nothing can resist, swept the race into a great but a very material civilization. This disappearance of the psychic faculties was quickened to some extent by the deliberate action of the higher and ruling classes in the Toltec empire of Atlantis. They deliberately for their own selfish purposes tried to dwarf, tried to stunt, the use of the psychic faculties in the lower classes of the popu-

lation, lower in evolution and therefore in the
social scale: and in order to make them more apt
instruments for their own purposes they used their
occult knowledge for the deliberate dwarfing of
their psychic faculties.  In this way the faculties
were artificially stunted in excess of the working
of the great kosmic law; and this makes me remind you of one thing that is worth thinking out
for yourselves at leisure.  That is, that no man can
resist the great sweep of kosmic law; no man can
stop the mighty march of the divine evolution; but
man may co-operate with it or work against it. He
may work for good or for evil. Recognizing the
wisdom and grandeur of the march he may work
with it for duty's sake and in submission to the
divine will; or he may try to grip for his own personal gain some of these forces of nature, and use
them for his own transient, for his own personal
and selfish gratification, instead of for the carrying
out of the divine purpose.  Where a man uses for
selfish purpose these great forces of the Kosmos
he makes his individual Karma bad, although the
tendency of the great Karma of the race remains
unaffected; thus the individual may mar his own
future; while he is within the wide sweep of the
kosmic law, he may make misery for himself in the
narrow circle of his own individual development;
for if he uses kosmic law selfishly he will reap a
selfish harvest, and so within this one great law
both happy and unhappy individual Karmas are

made. I say that, recommending it to you for detailed consideration, for it may solve for you some of the puzzles men often feel: how Karma can be a divine law by which man is swept onwards, seeming like a destiny imposed on him, while he yet knows that his own will is relatively free; he can choose his own path but within this mighty sweep.

As I say then, in that civilization of the past, man used this great law of the Kosmos for his own selfish purposes, and the final result was the destruction of Atlantis, the total sweeping away of that civilization, save for such wrecks of it as remained here and there in the world, especially in South America in the civilization of Peru, where some faint traces of its glory were left; so beautiful were these even in their degradation that when Peru was conquered by the Spaniards from the West they stood marvelling before the happiness of the community, before the sweetness, the gentleness, the purity of the people who lived there, the wisdom of the Government and the prosperity of the nation as a whole; that civilization which was slain by the Spaniards, trampled under foot by their advancing hosts, that was the last faint gleam of the civilization that I speak of which was so grand at its zenith, which had so great a fall, and was swept away by the catastrophe that made the Atlantic waves roll where once fair lands stretched.

Passing onward swiftly from that, we come to the evolution of our own race. To follow the re-

mainder of this evolution you must remember that
the Logos of our system reveals himself in threefold aspect. You know that in every great religion
the Trimûrti, or the Trinity, is the representation
of the manifested God; and you know also, at least
the more thoughtful and philosophic among you
know, that the Three are but a threefold manifestation of the One; the three aspects of the one un-
manifestated Existence, that can be known only
as it is manifested in the Universe. And you know
that in the threefold Logos there is seen the aspect
of Power, the aspect of Wisdom, the aspect of Love.

Now all human activities bear the impress of this
threefold Logos; all human activities may be classed under one or another of these headings—they
fall under the heading of power, of wisdom, or of
love, and under these three all races of men are
grouped, and all activities of nations and individuals are classed. I take that classification because
in a subject so complex as is mine this morning the
classification gives us a set of little boxes into
which you may put the different parts of the subject of the lecture for your further thought and
consideration. Remember that the three are one.
Remember that they interpenetrate each other. Remember that these divisions are divisions of phenomenal appearance and not of essence; but in-
as much as we are in the world of phenomena and
the separation is phenomenal, we may fairly take

it, and we shall not be misled by it if we realize the fundamental unity from which all proceeds.

Suppose then we take the threefold classification and sub-divide a little more: under Love we shall find those activities of mind will naturally fall which have to do on the one side with religion, on the other side with philanthropy, using both the words in their widest sense, religion meaning the service of those above us, philanthropy meaning the service of those around us and below us; so that under this one head of Love we include the whole of the human activities which pay homage and service to Those who are above us in evolution, and give help and compassion and assistance to all who are below and around us. Taking the division of the Gods and men, religion would have to do with the direct service of the Gods—and how much that means you will see in a few moments—while philanthropy would have to do with the direct service of men, in this physical plane at first, of the men we see around us. Under the heading of Wisdom will come all those activities of the human mind, both lower and higher, that we can divide further into science, philosophy and art. There we have three great fields of the activities of the mind that fall under the heading of wisdom; not that knowledge itself is wisdom, but it is the material out of which, by a spiritual alchemy, wisdom is evolved, for spiritually transmuted knowledge becemes wisdom; so we put all these activities of knowledge under the heading of wisdom as a whole. And then under the heading of Power will come all those human activities that have to do with the governing of man, with the exercise of administrative and executive functions, with the building of the nations, with the forming of communities, with everything in which power is exercised; and under this also come those creative faculties in man which are his by virtue of his birthright as the offspring of the Divine—those creative faculties that so few understand, that so few exercise with knowledge, which are the great means for human elevation, and the great force for human advance. All the efforts of the divine Teachers in the past and in the present are directed to bring these great fields of activity under intelligent human cultivation, so that they may be rightly tilled by man and that by such tillage his evolution may be ensured. All their efforts tend to give a right direction to these activities, that whether they be of love or of wisdom or of power, they may be sent along the right road for the general evolution of mankind. For this has every great religion been founded; for this has every noble code of morals been proclaimed; for this has every strong impulse towards intellectual development been intended; and for this in our own days is man given the fuller restatement of all the ancient truths, under that name of Divine Wisdom which, in its Anglicized Greek form, is now familiar to you as Theosophy.

It is but another re-statement of the old truth, another effort of the same Teachers to guide those activities of human life.

At the present time it is needed most especially; for if you look abroad in the world you will find that in each great department of human activity man seems to have come well-nigh to the limit of his powers. He has conquered the physical plane; he has so brought it into subjection that the physical is occupying far too much of his attention and interest, and the realities of the higher planes are veiled from his vision. If we look at the activities of life we find as to religion that materialism is fighting against it from one side and superstition is undermining it from the other; so that against religion there are turned two daggers in the hands of humanity, each of which is menacing its life— the scepticism that disbelieves, and the superstition that misbelieves. Both are fatal to human progress along this particular line of activity. When you turn from religion to philanthropy in the modern world, you find human misery too vast and too great for men to be able to grapple with it; where modern civilization is the most successful, where modern civilization is the most triumphant, there you find the greatest aggregate of suffering, and the most horrible misery which can crush human life; when you look at these miseries you not only see that philanthropy is helpless against them, but they are giving birth to resentment, to class hatred, to threats of revolution and anarchy. Thus civilization is menaced from its very foundation, and men know not how to meet the danger, for they have lost the spirit of love.

And if from love you turn to wisdom you find that there is difficulty everywhere in its three great fields. Science seems to have come to the end of its material resources. Its apparatus is so marvellously delicate that no further development seems within reach, its balance so marvellously accurate that it can weigh what seems an unperceivable part of a grain; and yet they say that there are substances imponderable even for their delicate balances. Science is almost at the end of its resources so far as its methods are concerned; and against its will it is being pressed upon by forces of a subtler and far more mysterious kind than it has been wont to recognize. If we look into the laboratory of the chemist, into the study of the scientific man, there seem to be pressing in forces that he cannot deal with by weight or measure; they puzzle him by their reality, while at the same time they are against every method of his science, they are against everything that he thinks he knows of nature. In philosophy you find the struggle between materialism which is proven to be inadequate and idealism which fails to find a steady and unassailable foundation; and you find also in the realm of art that art is tending to barrenness, to sterility, that no great new things are being produced but only inferior copies of the old; sterile, barren, it has lost its creative power.

And if you turn to the third great activity I have spoken of, the activity of power, what do you see in the modern world? Nation after nation trying experiments; they have lost the divine rulers that once were there, able to govern the nations and to guide them along the path of prosperity and of happiness; they are trying to make up for the loss of these divine kings by having a many-headed king that is called the People: instead of the divine kingship of mighty Initiates they have what is called self-government and the methods of democracy—as though by multiplying ignorance by a sufficiently big multiplier, you might be able to multiply it into knowledge. You find so far as the creative power is concerned that the very knowledge of it is gone, and people would be ridiculed who should speak of it, so far has man lost sight of his inheritance that is divine.

What does all this tell us? It tells us that mankind as a whole is going to take another step onwards. It tells us that we have reached one of those transition periods, where the old being outworn must give place to the new growth and the new development; under all the turmoil and the trouble, under all the distress and the perplexity, there are slowly forming within humanity the seeds of its next advance, which shall give back to these three great types of activity the ancient

power with a new development, the ancient definiteness with new lines of progress opening; for
while evolution does not go backward, retracing
its past steps and reproducing its ancient forms, it
goes on a spiral which reproduces on a higher level
all that was best on the lower; and upon such a
spiral humanity is treading now, to accomplish
with new powers and wider possibilities that which
in the past we see under different forms.

Consider love. When humanity takes its next
step upwards—and already there are signs here
and there that it is preparing for it—having made
the physical vehicle perfect, its work will be to perfect its second vehicle of consciousness, that in
which it is to function freely on the astral plane.
As thousands of years go by, mankind will develop
this second vehicle of consciousness, and the majority will be able to function in it on the astral
plane as easily and as readily as they function in
the physical body on the physical plane today.
Not quite the whole of mankind, for all men are
not equal, as the modern absurdity pretends; but
a great mass of men will take this step forward in
evolution, will develop that astral body and function in it completely, and so the progress of humanity will go on.

What difference will this step make? In religion
the open vision of humanity will bring within its
scope that plane of existence called the astral,
where many of the greater Intelligences manifest

themselves in form, for the helping and the teaching of men. Men will learn to see and know the Beings whose existence has been proclaimed to them by every mighty faith; they will know Them as now they know, or think they know, the physical bodies around them. They will know the beings of the at present unseen world. So that the majority of men will share with the advanced people of the present that first-hand knowledge that is now so rare, that first-hand certainty which will render scepticism for ever impossible. No man can be a sceptic as to the unseen world when he knows in his ordinary waking consciousness the existence of those beings surrounding us on every side, any more than you can be sceptical as to the existence of your fathers and mothers and your children. (I am not discussing the philosophic question of the Real and the Unreal; I am dealing with the phenomenal universe, and use words m the ordinary sense in which they are employed amongst us in our intercourse with each other.) When this step is taken, religion will so far change its character that that which is known and proclaimed by seers and prophets will be known by all men, and will be a matter within their experience and their daily cognizance, and the result will be that scepticism will be impossible, as it is impossible as regards much of the science of the present day. Superstition will be slain as much as scepticism. Superstition lives in darkness. It lives by human ignorance. It lives and grows and flourishes, and is a curse to the nations because some men who have the tradition of knowledge without its reality use that tradition for the enslavement of their fellow-men; and these, being ignorant, are terrified by the claim to knowledge and they bow down before those who assume to hold its keys, even though the keys be rusty and turn not in the locks at all. And we shall find, as you find today, that as men's eyes are opened superstition becomes impossible. You do not know the mischief that superstition works on the other side of death. You do not know the misery and the terror that too many souls undergo when they pass from the body into the world which to them is unknown, and is crowded for them with all the imaginary terrors with which superstition dominated by pretended knowledge has peopled it; especially is this the case in the West where men talk about eternal hell, and tell people that after death there is no growth and no progress, that a sinful man is plunged into the lake of fire and brimstone, there to spend the countless ages of eternity without hope of salvation, without hope of escape. You cannot imagine what the effect of that is on souls passing into the other world through the gateway of death, and imagining that all this is, or even may be true, imagining that they may be victims of this horror that they have heard of from their ignorant teachers; great are the difficulties they have who help the souls on the other side, to gradually do away with the terror and to make them understand that law is everywhere, and that malice and malignity are not found amongst the ruling powers of the Kosmos. So, as I say, scepticism will be impossible; superstition will be impossible; there will be other difficulties, other problems, other obscurities, but these twin enemies of man, scepticism and superstition, will be slain beyond resurrection when that day shall come for humanity.

And with love also on its philanthropic side the gain will be great; so much more can be done for man from that plane than from the physical. Physical activities make a great fuss, and have comparatively small results. You see a man running about making laws, and doing this and that in the world of the state and of society, and you think how great is his work, how wonderful are his results. But how small and petty they are in comparison with the results which flow from unseen labor done in quietness and silence, without speech of tongue, without effort of the physical body, done by the working of the mind in the subtler medium which affects men's thoughts more than their bodies, which influences their minds more than their outward frames. When humanity rises on to that higher plane, then this influence will be far more widely spread than it is today, and misery, crime and wretchedness will be met by working on the minds of men, purifying them and raising them, and thus lifting them above the possibilities that engulf them now. Do you realize, you to whom I am now speaking, that every one of you who generates an impure or revengeful or angry or sordid thought, sends out that thought into the world of society as a living force, as an active entity, which plays upon society, which is taken in by the weakest; by the most receptive, by the least developed, so that out of those thoughts of so-called respectable men there are scattered the seeds of crime through the lower masses of the pople, and the sins of these which show out in actions belong very largely to the Karma of those whose thoughts have given them birth. That is not known as widely as it should be known. It is not believed as it should be believed. Every man who feels revenge sends out into the astral world a power for destruction; and when some weak creature comes along with a bad Karma behind him, and bad circumstances surrounding him, with impulses which are not under his control and passions which are stronger than his mind, these evil thoughts come down upon him, all these angry thoughts from men living in respectable conditions in society, and if he be stimulated by some wrong, maddened by some injury, these impel him to strike a blow which we call murder; though he holds the knife in his physical hand, the blow is largely struck by the thoughts of many men whose revengeful feelings are of the essence of murder, although they appear not in outward form. You will not get rid of crimes in the lower strata of society until you purify the thoughts of the higher classes, of those who are educated and can understand the nature of things. And when all this is seen and known, when the astral world lies open to men's vision, there will be a new force available to help and to raise mankind; for men will no longer disbelieve in the power of thought, they will then appreciate their responsibility for the thoughts they generate, and will send out loving and helping influences instead of the degrading influences that go out so often today. Then also we shall find that direct help is possible, as it is indeed given now from that higher region; for the discoveries that men of science are making often come to them from that world by direct play on their minds. When a man of science takes a new departure, when a man, say like Sir William Crookes, discovers the genesis of atoms—one of the finest generalizations of modern science—do you think he has climbed up to that from below? I tell you that such ideas come from above and not from below. It is thus that the Teachers work on the minds of those who have some special capacity which is able to be utilized; and out of the world of thought, through the astral plane where thoughts are active functioning entities, they occasionally influence particular individuals in order that the progress of the world may be quickened and the growth of humanity may be facilitated. The reason why this is not done more frequently today is this: that until man's moral nature grows, it is not well that he should have too much knowledge of the unseen forces that lie behind the veil; he would misuse them instead of utilizing them, use them for oppression and for selfish purposes instead of for the lifting and helping of man. Therefore it is that knowledge is not more widely given; therefore it is that science is not more helped. Science, as one of the Great Ones said, must become the servant of humanity for it to receive very much help from Those who are above all else the Helpers and Saviors of the race.

In another way more rapid progress will be made in the days towards which we are looking. In education I suppose it has hardly struck you when dealing with children, when dealing with very young lads, how great are the possibilities that lie within them, if only their teachers had knowledge enough to directly foster the good and to dwarf and starve out the evil in them. You know that round every man there is visible to the trained eye, say to the eye of the Yogî, what is called an aura, which shows the development of the mind, the nature of the character, which gives definite information as to the stage of advancement reached by the soul that dwells in that body, and as to the characteristics and attributes of that soul. Every one of you bears around him this record of

his own state, the clearly seen evidence of the
stage that he occupies in evolution; round each
one of you there is this atmosphere that shows
your thoughts, that shows your character, that is
as legible to the trained eye as are the phyiscal
features to the physical eye, and is far more in-
structive as regards the character of the man. Now
when a young child comes into the world and
passes through the early stages of its growth, there
is this peculiarity about its aura: it brings with it
the karmic outcomes of its past, but a large number
of the mental and moral tendencies that it brings
over from the past are present in it in germ and
not in full fructification. If you take the aura of
a young child it is comparatively clean; its colors
are pure and transparent, not dense and muddy
and thick as they are in grown-up men and women;
within that aura lie the germs of tendencies which
may be developed. Some are good and some are
evil. The trained eye, distinguishing these characteristics, might cultivate the good and starve out
the evil by bringing suitable influences to bear on
the child. If you want a healthy plant from a seed,
you must take it and put it into good soil, and
you must water it and let the sunshine play on it.
All the essentials of the plant are in the seed, but
all the plant is not yet in manifestation, and according to the soil that you give it, the care you
take of it, the air that plays upon it, the sunshine
that warms it—according to these will be the

greater or the less development of the seed; it may be made to grow into great beauty or it may be stunted and dwarfed in its growth. So it is to a great extent with the little child. A child is born; it has in it the germ, say, of anger, of hot and passionate temper. Suppose that those around it are endowed with knowledge and wisdom, they will know how to deal with it. It should never be allowed to hear an angry word, it should never be allowed to see a passionate action. Every one around it should be gentle and loving and self-controlled; and there should never be sent to the germ that is within the child the stimulating force of the anger of older people that is like a force to make it grow more rapidly, to intensify it and force it to fructification. You should take care that round the children there should be influences that will stimulate all that is good, all that is noble, and all that is pure. And if you did that for every child humanity would go forward at a racing speed, whereas it goes forward with the gait of a cripple at the present time. Ignorance clouds men's minds and they know not how to train the young; there is failure round us, failure that will not exist when man rises to wider knowledge and educates by sight instead of blindly as he does today, educates with knowledge instead of ignorance. This need of real education explains why in the ancient days every boy was sent to a Guru. That ancient institution was meant to give to the

child the advantage of a trained mind playing on
his, and the help of an insight that went beyond
the insight of an ordinary man. The Guru used to
be a man who knew: the Guru used to be a man
who could see, and the child passed into his hands
because under such training the evil was dwarfed
and the good was developed. As the real Gurus
have gradually disappeared mankind has lost that
great advantage; but it will come back when
knowledge is spread amongst the people, and when
a higher stage of development makes this nobler
education possible.

All through the sphere of knowledge the methods
will be changed. The doctor will no longer be
obliged to guess at a disease from outside symptoms
but will diagnose by vision and not by reasoning;
men already are beginning to diagnose by the use
of what are called clairvoyant faculties; instead of
the doctor being shut out by the density of the
physical body, he utilizes the clairvoyant whose
sight pierces through physical matter, who can see
the disease, who can see exactly what is wrong
with any one of the organs of the body; he by this
vision, giving the necessary information to the doctor, enables him to act with perfect definiteness
and to trace the action of his drugs. Think how
different all medical science would be if the doctor
had that clairvoyant vision, and if what is now
held only by a few were generally spread amongst
them, so that they might diagnose with certainty

and trace the action of every remedy with the precision that comes from sight. So with chemistry how much more might the chemist do than he can today if his eyes were opened, how much more if he could trace all the stages of the combination of his materials, if he could make his compounds by vision instead of very often by guess-work, waiting for the result of an experiment before he is sure of the result coming about. How much of accident might be avoided, how much might this knowledge quicken the progress of science. A hint is given how such progress can be made in an article that can be found in the November (1895) number of *Lucifer*. You will see there how the limits of knowledge will enlarge when the mind has made manageable its vehicle upon the astral plane. And so with psychology: when men shall communicate with each other by thought instead of by the slow methods of pen and print, how thought will speed from brain to brain, communicating ideas without the clumsy processes that we use to-day. You will see at once what that means to humanity from the mere standpoint of this lower world. It means that separation will be a thing of the past, no mountain or sea will be able to divide man from man, friend from friend, relative from relative. It means that when men have conquered this region of nature they will be able to communicate with each other, mind with mind, no matter where they may travel, no matter in what land they may dwell; for to the mind there are no limitations of space and time as there are in the lower world. When man has perfected his astral vehicle he will always be within reach of those he loves, and separation will have lost its pain, as death also will have lost its power to divide. Take the life of man as it is to-day, take the life of nations as it is lived in the present, and you know that death and separation are two of the great sorrows that oppress humanity. Both of these will have lost their chief wounding power when man has taken this great step forward; both these will have lost their power to divide when man has reached that higher stage. That which only disciples have to-day shall then be shared by the majority; and how much fairer will be the lower life of man when these influences are swept away from disturbing him!

So also, of course, with philosophy with its then keener knowledge of the possibilities of matter and its then keener insight into the realities of life. So too with the writing of history, when all history shall be written from the âkâshic records and not in order to gratify the passions of a political party or to support some theory of human growth or to strengthen some hypothesis of scientific imagination. All history lies in the âkâsha; its records are there imperishable and indestructible; not one act of humanity that is past but is registered there, not one fact of human history that is not written there for the eyes that are able to see. The time will come when all history will be written from that, instead of in the ignorant way that it is written now, and men when they want to know the past will look back into the imperishable records and use them for swifter development, utilizing past experience to promote a swifter growth of humanity.

And what art will be when these new powers come within the reach of man, only those perhaps can estimate who to some extent use them now. Possibilities of new forms beautiful beyond expression, of colors dazzling beyond all imagination, colors unknown in the physical world, that take existence in the subtler matter of the astral plane— colors that none can describe because a color that is not known cannot be understood by verbal description. All those will come within the region of art, and all marvellous possibilities of the subtler senses.

And what of will and power? Then divine kingship will return to earth; then men will take their places in society according to the stage of development that they have reached, and not according to mere guess-work as they do to-day. All men will be able to see what they themselves and others are, for, printed on each man's aura, visible to all men's sight, will be his mental attributes and moral capacities, and therefore the place in human society that he is best fitted to take. Then we shall find young men trained for work for which their capacities fit them, for which their powers give possibility of achievement; there will not be the discontent there is to-day, for discontent arises out of faculties that are frustrated in their accomplishment and from a sense of injustice that works in the mind of men when they feel that they have powers and no opportunity of showing them, when they feel that they have capacities that they are not able to expand. If they were wise they would know, of course, that their circumstances were karmic. But now we are dealing with the masses, and not with the more thoughtful individuals. For them discontent will be impossible when each man is in the place for which his visible faculties fit him, and so there will be again a really orderly society. Then also we shall know better how to deal with the lower types of humanity. We shall not punish our criminals but cure them; we shall not slay them but educate them. We shall be able to see the very point at which help is needed; and there will be wisdom to reform instead of anger to punish. Not only will society change by thus working on the very natures of men, but all the outside world will also change its appearance; all the animal world will come under the moulding power of man. He will no longer be a tyrant and oppressor as he is now; but he will be a helper and educator and teacher of the lower animal world. He will do what he was meant to do—be the helper and the trainer of the brute, and not its ill-user and its oppressor, as he so largely is to-day. I need not say that all forms of cruelty will gradually fade away; no longer will animal blood stain the earth as it stains it so deeply now; no longer will animals fly from man with dread and horror, knowing him as enemy instead of recognizing him as friend; for we shall be passing onwards towards a golden age when all living things shall love instead of hate.

I have given you what seems a fairy tale, but it is only the next stage of man's growth, it is only the result of the conquest of the astral plane, of that which is next to the physical. What shall it be when man rises still higher, and occupies in full and waking consciousness the mânasic or mental plane? I can only take one or two of the points and show you how the expanding consciousness will triumph. If in those far-off days there should be an orator and an audience, how different then would be the oratory and how different would be the effect on the people. Instead of their hearing words, articulate sounds that reach the ears, and convey so imperfectly and inadequately but a small portion of the thought, they would see thought as it really is; thought springing out before their eyes radiant in color, beautiful in sound, exquisite in shape, and they would be spoken to as it were in music, they would be spoken to in color and in form, until the whole hall would be full of perfect music and perfect color and perfect shapes. For that is the oratory of the future when men have conquered that higher plane of consciousness and of life. Do you think I dream? I tell you there are those to-day who can go to that plane of consciousness and know it and feel it and see it, who are behind the veils that blind the majority and shut out from their view the wider possibilities of life. For as a man sanding on the top of a tower can see all the country round, and as from every part of the landscape there come to him colors and sounds and forms, but if he goes down the tower by the staircase he can only see as much of the landscape as a window in the wall may permit him to see: so is it with the life of man on the mental plane. Knowledge flows in to him on every side. Not through the senses as we know them, but through a single sense that answers to every vibration that comes from without. And as man goes down into the lower bodies it is just as though he descended into the tower; he can only see as much as the eyes and the ears and the nose—the little windows in the wall—enable him to know of the outside world; for the senses are only windows, and the wall of the body shuts us in, and only as we rise above the body are we able really to see the world around us in its glory, in its beauty and in its wonders.

Then again life will be so much mightier. All the greatest intellectual thoughts come from that region through the astral. The mightiest mental agencies for helping man in the physical world to-day are being sent down from the mânasic region by those who are able to function there. The disciples of the Masters are there in waking consciousness, working for the helping of man working for the raising of humanity; and every one who has passed those great portals of Initiation, about which yesterday I spoke to you, lives in that region working there for the helping of man. The disciple may work in the physical world; but he works far more in the higher and more effective region. There his greatest activities are carried on; there his furthest-reaching services are rendered. And when the majority of men rise to that region, how numerous will be the workers, how vast the congregation of the helpers! Only a few hundreds are functioning there to-day for the helping of the millions of mankind, and the work is imperfectly done because of the small number of the workers. But when the bulk of humanity rises there how swift will be the growth out of the lower stages of men. Mankind will be elevated with a speed that we can scarcely imagine to-day.

Higher yet and higher to another region that man shall conquer; that region where all is one and man knows himself as one with every manifested thing; the region called Turîya, which man shall occupy ere the Manvantara closes, that region which is now open to the waking consciousness only in the last stage of discipleship that I spoke to you about yesterday; into this the Seventh Race of men shall climb and this shall occupy. In that extended consciousness there is no separation that divides man from man; each knows himself to be

one with others; feels as they feel, thinks as they
think, knows as they know—a conscrousness that
stretches out to embrace myriads; and then the
brotherhood of man becomes an acuomplished fact.
There the essence of things is seen, and not only
the appearances; there realities are seen, and not
only phenomena. The one-Self is recognized that
lives in all; hatred is for evermore impossible to
the man who knows.

And above that still one step further, that no
words of mine can image, that no phrase of mine
can represent, that which the Sages have spoken
of as Nirvâna, which they have tried to explain and
have failed, because human language is inadequate
to the task, and from their efforts to impart their
own knowledge only misunderstanding has re-
sulted. It is consciousness so great that it is un-
imaginable, it is consciousness embracing the whole
universe and therefore seems as unconsciousness
to men's limited apprehension; but I tell you that
the life of Nirvâna, the life of the mighty Ones
that have attained it, is a consciousness beside
which our consciousness is as that of the stone, in
the limitations that bind it, in the blindness that
darkens it, and in the incapacity of its methods.
There is life there beyond all dreams of living, activity there beyond all possibilities of our thinking,
life which is one and yet that spreads itself forth in
manifested activities, where the Logos is the manifested Light, the beams whereof shine out through

all regions of the world. That too is man's goal for this Manvantara, that too he shall know when the Seventh Race has run its course, and the first fruits of our humanity who know it now shall find Themselves surrounded by countless myriads who then shall know it. Then the Life of the LOGOS for untold periods, then the perfect reflection of the LOGOS in Those who have grown into His image and likeness, until a new universe is to be born, until a new Kosmos is to come into activity. And These, in Their turn a LOGOS, shall build a new universe, shall train a new humanity. Such is the future that awaits us; such the glory to be revealed!

# THEOSOPHICAL PUBLISHING HOUSE

**American Branch**               **"Krotona"**

### Hollywood, Los Angeles, Cal.

The following books are selected from our catalogue, which contains the prices of books recommended:

## ELEMENTARY WORKS ON THEOSOPHY

Theosophy. Annie Besant.
The Riddle of Life. Annie Besant. (4 illustrations).
An Outline of Theosophy. C. W. Leadbeater.
A Textbook of Theosophy. C. W. Leadbeater.
The Ancient Wisdom. Annie Besant.

**THEOSOPHICAL MANUALS**
> The Seven Principles of Man. Annie Besant.
> Reincarnation. Annie Besant.
> Karma. Annie Besant.
> Death—and After? Annie Besant.
> The Astral Plane. C. W. Leadbeater.
> The Devachanic Plane. C. W. Leadbeater.
> Man and His Bodies. Annie Besant.

The Key to Theosophy. H. P. Blavatsky.
Esoteric Buddhism. A. P. Sinnett.
The Growth of the Soul. A. P. Sinnett.
Popular Lectures on Theosophy. Annie Besant.
Theosophy and the Theosophical Society. Annie Besant.
Theosophy Simplified. Irving S. Cooper.
A Study in Karma. Annie Besant.

## BOOKS ON THESOSOPHY AND RELIGIONS

A Universal Textbook of Religion and Morals. Annie Besant.
Fragments of a Faith Forgotten. G. R. S. Mead, B. A.
Esoteric Christianity. Annie Besant.
Four Great Religions (Hinduism, Buddhism, Zoroastrianism, Christianity). Annie Besant.
Is Theosophy Anti-Christian. G. Herbert Whyte.
The Christian Creed. C. W. Leadbeater.
Did Jesus Live 100 Years B. C.? G. R. S. Mead, B. A.
The Gospels and the Gospel. G. R. S. Mead, B. A.
The Esoteric Basis of Christianity. Wm. Kingsland.

# BOOKS ON THEOSOPHY AND ITS PRACTICAL APPLICATION

Thought Power; Its Control and Culture. Annie Besant.
In the Outer Court. Annie Besant.
The Path of Discipleship. Annie Besant.
The Ideals of Thesopohy. Annie Besant.
Some Problems of Life. Annie Besant.
Fragments of Thought and Life. Mabel Collins.
Theosophy and Life's Deeper Problems. Annie Besant.
Theosophy and the Problems of Life. A. P. Sinnett.

# BOOKS ON THEOSOPHY AND THE INNER LIFE

The Voice of the Silence. H. P. Blavatsky.
Light on the Path. Mabel Collins.
A Cry from Afar. Mabel Collins.
Love's Chaplet. Mabel Collins.
A Crown of Asphodels. Helen Bourchier.
The Doctrine of the Heart. Annie Besant.
Mysticism. M. Pope.
The Bhagavad Gita. Translated by Annie Besant.
One Life, One Law. Mabel Collins.
At the Feet of the Master. J. Krishnamurti.
Initiation: the Perfecting of Man. Annie Besant.
Mysticism. Annie Besant.
The Spiritual Life. Annie Besant.

# BOOKS ON THEOSOPHY AND SCIENCE

Theosophy and Modern Thought. C. Jinarajadasa.
The Physics of the Secret Doctrine. William Kingsland.
Scientific Corroborations of Theosophy. Dr. A. Marques.
Occult Chemistry. Annie Besant.
Nature's Finer Forces. Rama Prasad.
The Evolution of Life and Form. Annie Besant.

# BOOKS ON OCCULTISM

The Occult World. A. P. Sinnett.
In the Next World. A. P. Sinnett.
Dreams. C. W. Leadbeater.
Clairvoyance. C. W. Leadbeater.
Some Glimpses of Occultism. C. W. Leadbeater.
Man Visible and Invisible. C. W. Leadbeater.
Thought Forms. Annie Besant and C. W. Leadbeater.

(The last two richly illustrated with many colored plates)

Man: Whence, How and Whither? Annie Besant and C. W. Leadbeater.

Practical Occultism. H. P. Blavatsky.

## THEOSOPHY AND OCCULTISM IN FICTION

From the Caves and Jungles of Hindustan. H. P. Blavatsky.

The Perfume of Egypt. C. W. Leadbeater.

The Idyll of the White Lotus. Mabel Collins.

The Tear and the Smile. M. Charles.

The Ways of Love. Elizabeth Severs.

## BOOKS FOR CHILDREN

Chats with Colorkin. W. L. Hubbard.

Theosophy for Very Little Children. Clara M. Codd.

Talks with Golden Chain Links. Ethel M. Whyte.

Theosophy for Beginners. C. W. Christie.

Legends and Tales. Annie Besant.

The Great Teachers. G. Herbert Whyte.

In a Nutshell. Agnes Boss Thomas.

CPSIA information can be obtained at www.ICGtesting.com
Printed in the USA
LVOW09s2113290114

371471LV00001B/52/A